THE ALL-AMERICAN SPORTS FAN COOKBOOK

THE ALL-AMERICAN SPORTS FAN COOKBOOK

by
Elisa Garin
and
Cynthia Gomes

Peanut Butter Publishing
Seattle, Washington

Editor: Lindsay Aegerter
Cover Design: Jean Zaputil Sutphen
Illustrations: Copyright © 1988 by Jean Zaputil Sutphen
Typesetting: Laurel Strand

10 9 8 7 6 5 4 3 2

Published by Peanut Butter Publishing
329 Second Ave. W.
Seattle, WA 98119
(206) 281-5965

Contents

Dedication

This is dedicated to the men in our lives
who paint streets green for St. Patrick's Day
and like their Steak Tartar medium rare.

Introduction

From basketball to skiing, baseball to soccer, yachting to football, fans are hooked on the exhilaration, pageantry and camaraderie of sports.

For centuries, spectators have been drawn to demonstrations of skill, strength and valor. Historically, sports cookery has been an essential ingredient of the competition, whether it was selling spiced sausage at the Roman Coliseum or hawking pasties at a medieval tournament.

Certain foods have become synonymous with sporting events. What would baseball be without the hot dog, or Derby Day without the traditional mint julep? Sports fans vary in their interests, ages and affluence; however, food is the integral thread that ties groups as diverse as wrestling fans and yachting enthusiasts together.

Sports cookery changes with the action and the season. Tailgating for a cross-country ski trip may call for chili, crusty bread and red wine, while power boat competition on the lake is even more sensational with grilled Blue Cheese Burgers and Pazazz Potato Salad.

Theme parties work well for sporting events because they provide direction for planning, and they can be expanded or simplified depending on time and resources. The romantic Italian theme can be presented with something as simple as a candle and red-checked tablecloth, or more elaborately with strolling minstrels, tuxedoed waiters and Zabaione.

If the idea of setting up a Japanese tea garden in Dodger Stadium baffles you, consider Chinese take-out; it's convenient and won't cramp your style. Emphasizing seasonal foods such as fresh strawberries, spring lamb or garden vegetables can be the focus of a theme party. Do a fresh fruit salad bar for a summer swimfest or a crab feed for the football playoffs.

Unlike the conventional picnic carried in a wicker basket, tailgating facilitates sumptuous dining with an emphasis on space and mobility. Recently, we saw football aficionados pregame dining in a black limousine, table set with crystal, china and linen.

Tailgating, however, does not have to be a glamorous affair; a Texas barbecue in the back of a pickup truck or hearty soup and French bread served in wooden bowls are simple but satisfying alternatives.

Most avid tailgaters arrive early with plenty of time for set-up and pregame mingling. Getting an early start ensures organization, limits traffic congestion and avoids parking lot headaches. Lingering over chocolate torte and French roast coffee while recapping the game (pure decadence) has a distinct advantage in allowing time for traffic to clear before starting home.

Tickets are at a premium for Wimbledon or World Cup soccer, and the America's Cup is hard to view without a yacht. Television parties are the answer to front-row seats at these costly classics. The World Series, the Olympics and the Super Bowl are celebrated in homes across the nation as faithfully as Christmas and the Fourth of July.

Home-based parties provide a warm, casual atmosphere where friends can gather in the pursuit of good food, good grog and good times (the All-American way). Menus for home-based parties range from casual to sophisticated, from Louisiana barbecued shrimp and beer to chateaubriand and pinot noir.

Lacking space? Think about getting a group together and renting a suite in a luxury hotel; some hotels offer pregame packages that include barbecues, shuttle service and discounted room rates. Consideration is important at hotel parties; if your friends are too wild and crazy, perhaps they belong back in the tailgate section.

Sports cookery enjoys a long and savory history; it has influenced the overall atmosphere of sporting for centuries. Sometimes it is difficult to say whether the games influenced the food or the food influenced the games. But one thing is certain: Fine food and drink have contributed greatly to the enduring spectacle of sports and sports fans.

Our recipes are novel interpretations of familiar foods, new twists to old favorites. There are also many super, original creations such as Clam Fettucine and Borsch: The Beet-Um Soup.

The recipes are flexible, designed for anxiety-free cooking and sure to titillate the FUN HOG in all of us.

Equipment

Equipment can be simple or sophisticated, from Styrofoam coolers and prepackaged aluminum barbecues to portable Webers and well-stocked "traveling" bars.

Thermos containers come in all sizes and shapes; use them for everything from iced tea or sangria to sauces, soups, chilis and stews. If you use them for hot liquids, warm the thermos with hot water ahead of time.

Plastic zipped bags come in a variety of sizes and strengths; they are excellent for storing breads, salads and sandwiches, and you may want to fill them with ice and use them as "mini-coolers." Remember large garbage bags for bringing home trash, dirty dishes and the *cooled* grill.

Covered containers are convenient for transporting foods; make sure they are tightly sealed.

Dishes and utensils: Paper plates are practical, burnable and can be pleasing to the eye with the selection of styles and colors available today. Paper products come in all sizes and strengths. For more elaborate dining, there is clear plastic, stainless steel or china. This tableware can be costly, but it adds a touch of class to any sporting event. The same applies to utensils; stainless is more appealing than the plastic look.

Napkins: Your choice, paper vs. cloth. You may even consider disposable towelettes for those rib or chicken barbecues.

Glasses, mugs and cups: Better to use good quality Styrofoam for hot drinks to avoid leakage and burns, or get into the spirit of the occasion with your favorite souvenir team mug. Sturdy plastic works well for cold drinks, wine and beer, although we prefer the new, colored lucite glasses.

Coolers or ice chests are an absolute must! Not only do they store food and drink for hours, but they also provide large quantities of ice.

Seasoned sports fans come equipped with utility knife, can opener, corkscrew, serving spoons and forks, matches, and barbecue or camp stove. A checklist of the basics will help you "get it all together":

Food and Drink	Glasses, Mugs and Cups
Plates and Bowls	Table Cloth
Flatware	Serving Utensils
Napkins	Cutting Board

Tongs
Charcoal and Fire Starter
Matches
Spray Bottle
Condiments
Utility Knife
Can Opener
Paper Towels

Wipe Cloth
Ice
Ice Chest/Cooler
Garbage Bags
Kickback Chairs
TV (optional)
Radio (optional)

About Barbecuing

The days of rubbing two sticks together are long gone; there is nothing easier than grilling over a charcoal fire. You can make your fire with charcoal briquettes, with wood chips such as manzanita or mesquite, or with the new "charcoal bag" that requires only a match to light (fuel included in bag). There are several ways to fuel your fire: kindling, paper, electric starter or liquid starter. Please, read directions carefully and have a spray bottle at hand to control flames and heat intensity. Beginners tend to overload the barbecue with charcoal, creating an inferno; this is NOT the way to make blackened red fish. Cooking time will vary with the barbecue and the choice of fuel. Be sure to start your barbecue thirty to forty-five minutes ahead of planned cooking time.

Tips on Home-Based Parties

America loves a good party, especially when it focuses on sports. Success depends on pre-party planning and preparation. A well-designed party relieves pandemonium and will give you more confidence and ease. Keep in mind that your party will be as relaxed or as wild as you are. If the host or hostess is having fun, it is infectious and your good humor will set the tone of the celebration. So, by preparing dishes ahead of time (many recipes in our book fit this category) and setting up tables, chairs, bar and decorations in advance, you will be better organized and able to stay sane.

Choose a theme and work around it; appropriate party decorations set the atmosphere and signal the mood for a good time. Most party stores have many accessories: balloons, banners, streamers and favors suitable to most themes and occasions. Photographs, baskets, hats, festive table cloths, decorative fruits and autumn leaves or spring bouquets add a more personal, professional touch to your decorations.

Before deciding on your guest list, consider exactly how much space is available. Do not invite 150 people to your one-bedroom apartment. Make sure your friends are compatible but diverse; lively conversation is impossible when everyone is cut from the same mold. Buffets adapt well to crowds and dictate a more casual style of entertaining, but an intimate evening buffet after the Masters Golf Classic can become a dazzling affair with sterling, crystal and candlelight.

You should schedule your party around the time of the sports event you will be watching; decide whether your guests should arrive one to two hours or fifteen to twenty minutes before game time. If planning an outdoor barbecue, do not over-invite; summer thunder showers could force the gang indoors.

Select a menu that is within your capabilities. If you are basically a simple cook, do not choose a gourmet menu – it could become another "I Love Lucy" episode. If preparation time is precious, prepare recipes one to two days in advance. Always try to include an assortment of colors, textures and flavors; presentation is 50 percent of the overall effect. It is not necessary to serve several courses: fewer can be just as impressive with less work. Do have ample servings, but don't go overboard. Once you have decided on a menu, make a grocery list. Most of the ingredients listed in our recipes are readily available. Schedule your time so that everything is served together. Menu suggestions for home-based parties follow in this chapter.

Since home-based parties center around the televised event, determine where you want to set up televisions and make sure to hook up additional cable extensions in advance. We enjoy having them set up strategically so no one (not even the cook) misses the last-minute touchdown or the horse that wins by a nose. If you need more than one TV, borrow one from a friend. For the ultimate in sports television, and if weather permits, put the TV outside on a deck or in a shaded area and line up the lawn chairs; no need to be indoors on a beautiful day.

Theme Parties

There are books written on theme parties, but if this is your first, choose a cuisine that interests you; look around the house for props and recipes you'd like to try. If you've always wanted to try Thai cooking, make a trip to the library and bookstore to read up on Thai cookery and customs. Check your area for Thai stores or delis as resources for decorations and ingredients. Take time to try your new recipes on family and friends. To ensure authenticity, invite a native of Thailand to test your recipes. Theme parties can be as extravagant as a traditional Scandinavian buffet after a day of Nordic skiing, or as simple as a Cinco de Mayo celebration of tacos and Mexican beer.

Theme parties need not be based on foreign cultures; they may simply relate to the sports event: hot dogs for baseball, barbecue for rodeo, quiche for polo. Period pieces such as a 1950s Bop Party or a 1960s Love-In are great ideas, especially when teamed with classic cars and music. A Great Gatsby lawn party or an Esther Williams swimfest is an original theme for summertime parties. Another easy way to create a theme is to decorate with color; invite guests to wear team colors, and accent your home accordingly.

Decorations and props can be found everywhere. The more creative you are in your search for them, the more interesting your party will be. For a boating party, check your local marine supply for nets, flags, nautical brass, etc. Planning a good theme party can be as much fun as giving one. Check the following menu suggestions for more ideas.

Menu
Suggestions

Tex-Mex Baja 500 Buffet

Margaritas
Ceviche   Scratch Bean Dip   Guacamole
Tortilla Chips

Artichoke Salad   Fruit and Yogurt Salad
Gaspacho Molded Salad

Very Original Tamale Pie   Los Lobos Casserole
Green Chili Rice   Turkey Enchiladas

Homemade Ice Cream with Grand Marnier Sauce

Spiced Coffee

Strictly Seafood

Sea Sips

Stuffed Mushrooms   Salmon Cheese Ball
Shrimp Dill Dip
with
Wafers and Baguettes

Carrot Grape Slaw   Crab Halibut Casserole
Cold Pasta Salad

Pregame Brunch

Sunday Morning Wakeups

Moch Caesar Salad   Ham Paté

Seafood Florentine

Victory Muffins with Sweet Butter

Scratch Cheesecake

Frozen Peach Daiquiris

Summer Barbecue

Denver Orange Crush Cocktail

Leaf Lettuce with Bayou Blue Cheese Dressing
Spinach Garbanzo Salad

Barbecued Butterflied Leg of Lamb
Louisiana Barbecued Shrimp
Zucchini Tomato Sauté

French Bread and Butter

Strawberry Zabaione

Oriental Special

Wontons with Chutney Dip
Japanese Vegetable Pickles

Chinese Salad Dressing with Raddiccio

Whole Stuffed Barbecued Fish   Ginger Soy Chicken
Classic Japanese Curry

Date Nut Cake
Green Tea

Sandwich Bar for a Crowd

Stands Fans Submarines   Crab Carries
Italian Turkey Sandwiches   Barbecued Fajitas

Dublin Potato Salad

Fresh Fruit

Sodas, Iced Tea and Imported Beer

Tailgate

Butter Lettuce with Curry Dill Dressing
Pazazz Potato Salad

Tailgate Chateaubriand   Arts, Zukes and Toms

Garlic Bread

Fresh Fruit in Champagne

Finger Foods Only

Stuffed Grape Leaves
All-American Paté

Frittata d' Artichokes
Spicey Drummettes

Salmon Cheese Ball with Assorted Crackers
Herb Curry Dip
Stuffed Pasta Shells

Picnic

Spinach Balls   Brandied Almonds
Radish Dip

Tabuli Salad
Mixed Greens with Seafood Salad Dressing

Chicken with Beer Marinade
Italian Stuffed Eggplant

Pineapple Cake

Cranberry Champagne Cocktail
Rose Cooler

Hockey Night Out

Spicey Drummettes   Oyster Spread with Wafers

Italian Potato Salad

All in One Sandwiches
Barbecued Lima Beans

Health Nut Cake

Hot Lemon Brandy

APPETIZERS
AND DIPS

Shrimp Remoulade

¼ c Dijon-style mustard
½ c vinegar
2 T catsup
1 T chili powder
¼ tsp cayenne pepper
3 cloves garlic (crushed)

¼ tsp dry tarragon
¾ c oil
½ c green onions (chopped fine)
½ c celery (chopped fine)
1½ lbs boiled shrimp or prawns

In a food processor or blender combine mustard, vinegar, catsup, chili powder, cayenne, garlic and tarragon. Slowly add the oil until it is totally incorporated into the mixture. Pour into a bowl and add onions and celery. This sauce may be served over shrimp as a cocktail or beside as a dip.

Stuffed Mushrooms

Makes: 20 caps

2 lbs or about 20 large
   mushrooms
½ c onion (grated)
4-5 cloves garlic (crushed)
2-3 T butter or margarine
¾ c dry bread crumbs
2 cans smoked oysters (drained
   and coarse chopped)

4 T parsley (chopped fine)
½ tsp salt
½ tsp pepper
½ tsp basil
⅓ c Parmesan cheese

Wash mushrooms and remove stems. Arrange caps on an ungreased baking sheet and set aside. Chop stems and sauté in a skillet with onion, garlic and margarine. Cook until lightly browned. Add remaining ingredients except cheese and cook an additional 5 minutes. Blend in cheese and spoon mixture into mushroom caps. Bake at 350 degrees for 15-20 minutes. Remove and serve hot or cold.

Variation: Substitute cheese-flavored cracker crumbs for dry bread crumbs.

Ceviche

2 lbs raw tuna or striped bass
  (cleaned and deboned)
1 c fresh lemon juice
1 c fresh lime juice
^{2}/$_3$ c olive oil
^{1}/$_2$ medium red bell pepper
  (chopped)
^{1}/$_2$ tsp dried basil (crumbled) or
  10 fresh basil leaves

1 tsp salt
^{1}/$_2$ c green onion (chopped)
2 tomatoes (chopped)
4 dashes Tabasco
3 T cilantro (chopped)
^{1}/$_4$ tsp white pepper

Cut fish diagonally, across grain, and into thin strips. Combine remaining ingredients and pour over fish. Marinate at least 2-3 hours before service. Serve with French bread or over butter lettuce salad.

Honey Ginger Meatballs

Makes: 30-40 1 inch meatballs

1^1/$_2$ lbs lean ground beef
1 large egg
1 c bread crumbs
1 tsp salt
2 tsp Worcestershire sauce
2 T vermouth
3 cloves garlic (crushed)

^{1}/$_4$ c soy sauce
^{1}/$_4$ c honey
^{1}/$_2$ tsp ground ginger or 1 T fresh
  grated
^{1}/$_2$ tsp pepper
1 c flour

Combine all ingredients except flour in a mixing bowl and form into 1 inch balls. Roll meatballs in flour to coat lightly. (This helps them stick together better.) Place in a baking pan and cook at 350 degrees for 18-20 minutes. Wrap and serve hot or cold at game time with sauces such as lemon horseradish, mustard or sweet and sour. For recipes see Sauce Section. These are perfect no-fuss appetizers because they can be premade and frozen or refrigerated until needed. For barbecue they may be skewered and reheated or made into sandwiches.

Wrapped Asparagus

1 lb or 12 fresh asparagus spears
12 thin slices turkey, ham,
    Prosciutto or salami
1 egg
1-2 T vinegar
2 tsp Dijon-style mustard
1 clove garlic (crushed)

¼ tsp salt
⅛ tsp pepper
1 tsp Worcestershire sauce
2 T cilantro or watercress leaves
    (optional)
½ c cottage cheese
½ c salad oil

Steam asparagus until tender and wrap with your choice of thin sliced cold meat. In a blender or food processor blend remaining ingredients (except oil) until smooth. With blender running, gradually add oil in a constant stream until smooth. This sauce can be poured over wrapped asparagus or served separately as a dip.

Variation: We have also served these hot by broiling the wrapped asparagus for 2-3 minutes then serving over rice with heated sauce. It's an elegant item in any case. Or substitute poached Dover sole for meat.

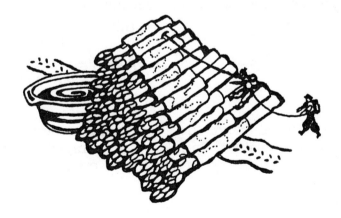

All-American Paté

2 lbs raw chicken livers
1 c chicken broth
8 slices uncooked bacon
1³/₄ c onions (chopped fine)
5 hard boiled eggs (chopped)
3 T butter or margarine
1 T salt

1 tsp pepper
2 tsp curry powder
2 dashes nutmeg
2 T parsley
1 tsp thyme
2 T scotch, brandy or dry sherry

In a saucepan, simmer chicken livers and broth for about 15 minutes, then drain. In a skillet, cook bacon until crisp. Remove bacon, drain and chop. Retain bacon drippings and sauté onion until transparent. Remove with a slotted spoon. Combine livers, bacon, onions and remaining ingredients in food processor. Process for about 5 minutes or until fairly smooth. Refrigerate until ready to serve. If you have a mold, firmly pack paté into a buttered 1 qt mold, then chill until firm. To serve, loosen edges with a knife. Invert onto a lettuce-lined tray and serve with sliced baguettes, crackers or cocktail breads.

Salmon Spread

2 (8 oz) pkg cream cheese
    (softened)
2 (4 oz) cans salmon (drained
    and boned)
¹/₄ c vermouth

4-5 stuffed green olives (chopped)
1 T onions (minced)
¹/₂ tsp tarragon
¹/₂ tsp Parmesan cheese

Mix together softened cream cheese, salmon, vermouth, olives and onion in a covered container. Sprinkle with tarragon and Parmesan cheese. Refrigerate until ready for use. Serve on crackers or French bread slices.

Variations:
1. Substitute a 2 oz can of finely chopped anchovies for salmon.
2. For more of a dip consistency add 8-10 oz sour cream to the above recipe.

Frittata d' Artichoke
Serves: 6-8

2 (6 oz) jars marinated artichoke hearts or mushrooms
1 small onion (chopped)
1 large clove garlic (crushed)
3 c fresh or 1 (10 oz) pkg frozen broccoli (chopped)
5 eggs (beaten)
4-5 soda crackers (crushed)
¾ tsp basil
¼ tsp thyme
¼ tsp oregano
1 tsp white wine Worcestershire sauce
½ tsp chervil
1 tsp salt
½ tsp pepper
2 c Mozzarella or Provolone cheese (grated)

Drain oil from artichokes into a skillet. Sauté onion and garlic in oil until tender. Add broccoli and reduce heat to low for about 3 minutes. Coarse chop artichokes. In a mixing bowl, combine eggs, cracker crumbs, sautéed vegetables, artichokes, spices and cheese. Pour mixture into a greased baking dish 9 x 13 inches and bake at 350 degrees for 25-35 minutes or until firm throughout. Cut into portion sized pieces. This item is very good either hot or cold and it travels well.

Variations:
1. Substitute thinly sliced zucchini or fresh spinach for broccoli.
2. Add bacon crumbs, ham chunks, cooked potato cubes or sliced mushrooms.

Shrimp and Crab Filled Biscuits
Makes: 10

1 (10 oz) pkg refrigerator biscuits
1 (6 oz) can shrimp (drained)
1 (6 oz) can crab (drained)
2 eggs (beaten)
1 c Fontina or Monterey Jack
   cheese (grated)
¼ c Ricotta cheese

½ c green onion (chopped)
¼ c mushrooms (chopped)
¼ c Parmesan cheese
2 T fresh parsley (chopped fine)
salt and pepper to taste
pinch of cayenne pepper to taste

Grease a muffin pan and separate biscuits. Press each biscuit into muffin pan (about ¼ inch thick) and set aside. In a mixing bowl, combine remaining ingredients. Spoon into biscuits and bake about 20 minutes at 375 degrees or until filling is firm but lightly browned. Cool about 10 minutes and remove from muffin pan. Or wrap and take to game hot. These are excellent used for brunch or beside a soup or stew. And in the tin they would travel well!

Variation: Substitute cooked sausage, chorizo or salmon. You may want to add some chopped green or black olives, just because.

Avocado Stuffed Celery
Serves: 8

1 avocado (mashed)
2 cloves garlic (crushed)
1 T lemon or lime juice
2 dashes Tabasco sauce

½ tsp cilantro (chopped fine)
salt and pepper to taste
1 bunch celery (cut into sticks)

In a medium mixing bowl, combine first 6 ingredients and mix until smooth. Stuff celery, package and keep chilled till gametime. May be garnished with crumbled bacon or diced tomato.

Spicey Drummettes

4 lbs chicken drummettes
2 T butter or margarine
½ c brandy or scotch
5 T chili sauce
2 (juice of) freshly squeezed
  lemons
1 tsp crushed red peppers

2 T oyster sauce
1 tsp basil
½ tsp rosemary
½ tsp ginger
4 cloves garlic (crushed)
salt and pepper

Can be done in oven or barbecue.

Oven Method: Wash and pat drummettes dry. Arrange on buttered baking dish. In a saucepan, mix remaining ingredients and simmer for 15 minutes. Pour over drummettes and bake 40 minutes, basting occasionally. Great hot or cold.

Barbecue Method: Wash and pat drummettes dry. Arrange in buttered baking dish and cook for 15-20 minutes at 325 degrees. In a saucepan, mix remaining ingredients and simmer for 15 minutes. Refrigerate precooked drummettes in this marinade until ready to barbecue. Barbecue as desired using extra marinade to baste during cooking.

Brandied Almonds

4 c unsalted almonds, peanuts,
  cashews or walnuts
¼ c butter or margarine

3-4 T brandy, rum or amaretto
½ c sugar
salt to taste

Sauté nuts in butter over low heat, stir in liquor and sugar, then sauté until golden brown. Drain on paper towels and salt to taste. Store in a covered container for several days before service.

Stuffed Grape Leaves

Filling

¼ c vegetable oil
2 c onions (chopped)
1½ c rice (uncooked)
⅓ c lemon or lime juice
½ c cilantro (chopped)
2 tsp salt

¾ tsp pepper
4 oz tomato sauce
1 clove garlic (crushed)
1 tsp Italian seasoning
1½ c dry white wine

One Day Before: In a large nonstick skillet, sauté onions in oil until tender. Add remaining ingredients and bring to a boil. Let simmer, stirring frequently until all liquid has been absorbed (15-20 minutes). Refrigerate rice mixture overnight so it is cool enough to handle.

Next Day: The number of grape leaves depends on how many you want to make. Probably about 50-60 fresh or 1-2 jars of canned. If canned grape leaves are used, omit the salt in filling. With fresh leaves just wash. Pinch off stems and place leaves on a clean surface, stem side up and toward you. Place 1 T of filling in the center of each leaf, fold over sides and roll leaves into a cigar shape. Line the bottom of a covered casserole with a layer of loose grape leaves and place rolled leaves into pan, seam side down. Tightly layer leaves until you run out of filling. Place a layer of loose leaves on top. This will help keep the outer layers from over-cooking. Pour 2 c water and ¼ c lemon juice over leaves and bake at 350 degrees for about 1½ hours. Refrigerate grape leaves until service. These are generally eaten with the fingers and can be served out of the baking dish or arranged on platters. They are really a novel appetizer and can be made up a few days ahead.

Variation: This filling can also be used to stuff bell peppers, tomatoes and eggplant.

Ham Paté

1³/₄ lbs ground ham (have
   butcher grind)
1³/₄ lbs lean ground pork
3 slices bread
1 onion (finely chopped)
2 eggs (lightly beaten)
½ tsp Italian seasoning
2 dashes Tabasco
½ tsp parsley
½ c milk
¼ c Madeira wine

Basting Sauce
½ c brown sugar
1 T dry mustard
¼ c vermouth
2 T water

Horseradish Sauce
¼ c prepared horseradish
1½ T Parmesan cheese
1½ T vinegar
pepper to taste
½ c sour cream
1 tsp chervil

Place ham, pork, bread, onion and eggs into a mixing bowl. Add remaining paté ingredients and mix thoroughly. Shape into loaf, place in roasting pan and score deeply. Bake at 350 degrees for 1 hour. Combine ingredients for glaze and use to baste loaf while cooking.

Blend ingredients for horseradish sauce and chill until service. Paté may be served hot or cold with horseradish sauce beside. A mustard or caper sauce would be great also.

Spanokopita Squares

Makes: 60 1½ inch squares or 10-15 pockets

3 lbs or about 4 bunches fresh
 spinach
2 bunches green onions (chopped)
2 T olive or grape oil
½ c parsley (finely chopped)
2-3 tsp dill weed
1 tsp basil

8 eggs (beaten lightly)
1 lb crumbled Feta or Monterey
 Jack cheese
salt to taste
½ to 1 lb Phyllo dough (check
 your deli or gourmet shop)
olive or grape oil

Cut spinach into 2 inch lengths and wash. Sauté onions in 2 T olive oil until almost brown. In a saucepan of boiling water, steam spinach slightly, cool and drain. Combine cool spinach, parsley, dill, basil, eggs, onions, cheese and salt to taste. Mix ingredients well.

Instructions for making squares: Butter a 13⅓ x 8¾ inch pan. Alternate layers of Phyllo dough and filling until mixture is gone. Cover top with sheet of Phyllo and brush with oil. Bake at 350 degrees for 30-45 minutes or until lightly browned. Cut into 60 1½ inch squares. May be served hot or cold. Can be prepared ahead and refrigerated for cooking or service.

Instructions for making pockets: Thaw Phyllo dough if frozen and wrap dough in a damp cloth as it dries out easily. Remove 1 sheet of dough and brush with oil. Cut into quarters. Spoon filling into the middle of one edge of each and fold into a rectangular or triangular pocket. Brush pocket with oil or it will not brown and crisp. (It will end up dry as a wall mat.) Bake as directed above.

Stuffed Pasta Shells

1 (8 oz) pkg large shell macaroni
1/4 lb crab
8 oz cream cheese (softened)
1 tsp curry
1/4 c green onion (chopped)

1/3 c Parmesan cheese
3 T parsley (chopped fine)
3 cloves garlic (crushed)
1/2 c Ricotta cheese

Cook macaroni shells as directed on package then drain and rinse with cold water. Do not overcook or they get sort of limp!!! No further comment. Set aside. Combine remaining ingredients, mixing well. Carefully spoon this mixture into shells as a filling. Refrigerate until ready to serve. May be garnished with pimiento, fresh dill sprigs or green olive slices.

Variation: Drizzle with Italian dressing and serve on a bed of lettuce or spinach leaves as an individual salad. These can also be used in antipasta trays with fresh veggies, olives and deli meats.

Artichoke Bites

1 (24 oz) jar marinated artichoke hearts
1 pkg frozen prepared puff pastry
4 oz blue cheese (crumbled)

Drain artichoke hearts thoroughly. Roll out puff pastry and cut into 3 inch squares. In the middle of each square add 1 heart and a pinch of blue cheese. Bring all four corners together and pinch closed. Arrange bites on a lightly greased cookie sheet 1/2 inch apart. Bake for 10-15 minutes at 375 degrees. These can be served hot or cold and are fabulous.

Brandy Mushrooms

Makes: 1½-2 c

4 cloves garlic (crushed)
¼ c butter or margarine
2 T vermouth
1 T brandy
¼ tsp almond extract
1 T Worcestershire sauce

1 T lemon juice
1 T parsley (chopped)
¼ c sliced almonds
½ lb fresh mushrooms
salt to taste

Combine all ingredients in a skillet (except mushrooms) and simmer for 10 minutes. Add mushrooms and simmer an additional 10 minutes. These are terrific on top of barbecue beef or lamb.

Vinaigrette for Vegetables

Makes: 1½ c

The vegetables used are your choice, however, ideas include broccoli, cauliflower, cabbage pieces, snow peas, zucchini, string beans, baby artichokes, carrots, mushrooms, red and green bell pepper or jicama. Try what you like, either raw or steamed ever so slightly, then add to the marinade below.

Dressing

½ c olive or vegetable oil
1 c vinegar
3 cloves garlic (crushed)
¼ c lemon or lime juice
1 tsp paprika

1 tsp oregano
1 tsp rosemary
½ tsp basil
½ tsp savory
salt and pepper to taste

Combine marinade ingredients and pour over vegetables. Chill 3-4 hours in a covered container. To serve, arrange vegetables on a serving platter and drizzle with extra marinade. Garnish with chives. May be used with imported cheeses, sliced baguettes or crackers.

Salmon Cheese Ball

Makes: 1 cheese ball

2 c cooked salmon (or a 1 lb can)
8 oz cream cheese (softened)
1 T lemon juice
1 green onion (chopped fine)
1 tsp prepared Dijon-style
  mustard

1 tsp prepared horseradish
1/4 tsp thyme
1/4 tsp Liquid Smoke Flavor
1/2 c walnuts (chopped)
3 T parsley (chopped)

Flake salmon, removing skin and bones, and combine with next 6 ingredients. Mix thoroughly and shape mixture into a ball or mold. Roll ball into parsley and nuts. Refrigerate overnight and serve with crackers, French bread, etc.

Oyster Spread

Makes: 2 c

2 cans smoked oysters (drained
  and chopped)
1/4 c green onions (chopped)
1 (8 oz) pkg cream cheese
  (softened)

1 (8 oz) pkg sour cream
1/4 tsp cayenne pepper
1 clove garlic (crushed)

Combine all ingredients in a covered container and chill until service. This is a sinful spread that is wonderful on thinly sliced baguettes or English wafers. Indulge!!

Spinach Balls

2 pkg (10 oz each) frozen chopped
   spinach
1 1/2 c bread crumbs
3/4 c Parmesan cheese
1 cube butter or margarine
3 green onions (chopped fine)

4 eggs
1 tsp thyme
1/2 tsp sage
dash of nutmeg
salt and pepper

Serve with Mustard Sauce: Page 140

In a mixing bowl, combine all ingredients and mix well. Shape into 1 inch balls and refrigerate or freeze until ready to bake. Place balls on an ungreased baking sheet and cook for 10-15 minutes at 350 degrees, until light brown. Wrap and serve hot or cold. Have mustard sauce available for a dip. These are easy and can be made ahead, then cooked when needed.

Tex-Mex Tostada Dip

Serves: 10-12

2 (1 lb) cans refried beans
3-4 mashed avocados
1 T lemon or lime juice
1 clove garlic (crushed)
salt and pepper to taste
1 1/2 c sour cream

1/2 c Cheddar cheese (grated)
1-2 medium tomatoes (chopped)
3-4 green onions (chopped)
3/4 c fresh or prepared salsa
1 can pitted black olives
1 (16 oz) bag tortilla chips

Spread beans 1/2 inch thick on platter. Mix avocado, lemon juice, garlic, salt and pepper. Spread avocado mixture over beans and top with layers of sour cream, cheese, tomatoes, onions and salsa. Garnish with whole olives and serve with tortilla chips.

Homemade Mexican Salsa

Makes: 2½ c

2-3 cloves garlic (crushed)
½-1 yellow or green fresh
   jalapeño chile pepper
salt and pepper to taste
4-5 fresh large tomatoes (peeled,
   cored and chopped)

2 (4 oz) cans diced green chiles
2 T vinegar
1-2 T oil
4 green onions (chopped)

Mix all ingredients in a covered jar, refrigerate overnight. Adjust salt, pepper and chiles to taste. My brother likes suicidal salsa, whereas I prefer to maintain the integrity of my tonsils. Either way, it's wonderful.

Variations:
1. Add ½ bunch chopped cilantro to salsa.
2. Where available, Cynthia adds a bit of prepackaged "menudo" spices just for flavor. Check specialty shops or Mexican markets.

Savory Garlic Dip

Makes: 1½ c

1 pkg (8 oz) cream cheese
   (softened to room temp)
½ c mayonnaise
2 T chives or green onion
   (chopped)
¼ tsp red peppers (crushed) or
   ⅛ tsp cayenne pepper

½ tsp salt
1 T lemon juice
¼ tsp savory
1 T sesame seeds
3-4 cloves garlic (crushed)

Combine all ingredients in a small bowl and mix well. Place in a covered container and chill until service.

Lemon Cilantro Dip

Makes: 1½ c

1 c cottage cheese
8 oz cream cheese (softened)
juice of 1 large fresh lemon
2 T dry white wine
½ tsp dried mustard

1 T sesame seeds
¼ tsp salt
2 tsp fresh grated lemon rind
¼ c fresh cilantro (chopped fine)

In a food processor or blender, combine cottage cheese, cream cheese, lemon juice and white wine until smooth. Stir occasionally to keep mixture from clumping. In a small bowl, blend cheese mixture and remaining ingredients. Refrigerate until service. Very good served with boiled prawns, French bread slices or as a dip for meats and raw vegetables. This is luscious for cilantro lovers and is a light, flavorful dip.

Spinach-Yogurt Dip

Makes: 1½ c

1 (10 oz) pkg frozen chopped
   spinach
2 T olive or vegetable oil
¼ c onion (chopped fine)
1 c plain yogurt
4 oz Feta cheese (crumbled)
2 cloves garlic (crushed)
1 tsp fresh mint leaves (chopped)
   or ½ tsp dry mint leaves

¼ tsp Lawry's seasoning salt
¼ tsp dill
⅛ tsp white pepper
1 tsp lemon juice
2 T almonds, pecans or walnuts
   (chopped fine)

Thaw and squeeze excess liquid from spinach. Chop fine. In frying pan, heat oil and cook onion until tender. Stir in spinach and sauté for 2 more minutes before removing from heat. Combine spinach mixture with remaining ingredients until thoroughly blended. Cover and refrigerate until ready for service. Serve with raw vegetables or with French bread or crackers.

Wontons with Chutney Dip

Makes: 2 c

1½ c cider vinegar
1 c plum sauce
¾ c chutney
1 tsp hot mustard

¼ tsp fresh ginger (grated)
1 (14 oz) pkg wonton skins
oil for deep frying
1-2 green onions (chopped)

Combine first 5 ingredients in a pan and cook over medium-low heat, stirring constantly until bubbly. Remove sauce from heat. May be made several days ahead and refrigerated. Reheat and place in a thermos till game time.

Wontons: Heat oil in a wok or deep skillet at about 375 degrees. Add wontons in batches, frying until golden or about 2 minutes. Drain on paper towel.

To serve: Pour sauce into bowl and garnish with sliced green onions. Arrange fried wontons on the side.

Variation: Use crackers topped with cream cheese. Spoon chutney sauce on top.

Artichoke Dip

Makes: 3 c

2 jars marinated artichoke hearts
  (drained and chopped)
½ c sour cream
¼ c parsley (chopped)
1 T lemon juice
1 tsp dill weed

1 tsp salt
½ tsp pepper
1 (8 oz) pkg cream cheese
1 green onion (chopped)
2 cloves garlic

Combine all ingredients in food processor or blender and blend well. Put in a covered container and chill overnight and until game time. Wonderful served with crackers or baguettes.

Crab and Cheese Dip

Serves: 8

Serve hot in a fondue pot.

¾ lb fresh cooked or 2 cans crab meat (drained)
¾ lb Cheddar cheese (grated)
1 (4 oz) can mild green chiles (chopped)
½ tsp dry mustard
1 clove garlic (crushed)
½ can of beer

Combine ingredients and melt over heat, stirring occasionally. When thoroughly blended, serve fondue-style with sliced or cubed French bread. Stir occasionally during service.

Scratch Bean Dip

Makes: A lot!!

1 lb dry pinto beans
5 c water
1 medium onion (chopped)
1 (8 oz) can tomato sauce or
  (12 oz) can tomato paste
1 (4 oz) can green chiles (chopped)
  or 1-2 fresh jalapeño peppers
1-2 slices bacon (cooked and
  crumbled)

2 bay leaves
2 tsp powdered cumin
2-3 cloves garlic (crushed)
2 T chili powder or paste
2 tsp oregano or 2 tsp menudo mix
½ c Monterey or Cheddar cheese
  (grated)

Bring beans to a boil for 4 minutes then let soak for 1-2 hours. Add onion, tomato sauce, chile peppers, bacon, bay leaves, cumin, garlic, chili powder and oregano. Simmer beans slowly until very soft. Drain cooking liquid from beans into a separate bowl and using a food processor or potato masher, crush beans. Use the cooking liquid to bring mashed bean mixture to a dip consistency. Bean dip may be served hot or cold topped with cheese and rolled flour tortillas or tortilla chips on the side. May be garnished with chopped green onions, olives and tomatoes. This is a dip that travels well and can be assembled quickly to stave off the hungry mob.

Skinny Dip

Makes: 3 c

10½ oz tofu (drained)
1 c plain unflavored yogurt
1 c raw mushrooms (chopped)
½ tsp Italian seasoning
1½ tsp Worcestershire sauce
½ tsp chili powder
½ tsp salt
1 tsp prepared Dijon-style
   mustard

2 T lemon or lime juice
1 green onion (chopped)
¼ c carrot (grated)
1 T prepared horseradish
1 (10½ oz) can baby clams
   (drained)
Tabasco to taste

Combine tofu and yogurt in food processor or blender until smooth. In a mixing bowl, blend with remaining ingredients. This is a dieter's delight with raw vegetables. Try it — you'll be surprised. The fussiest eater won't realize it's healthy.

Guacamole Dip

Makes: 1½ c

2-3 large avocados (mashed)
3 T prepared or homemade salsa
4 drops Worcestershire sauce
2 cloves garlic (crushed)
1 tsp lemon or lime juice

salt and pepper to taste
tortilla chips
crumbled bacon and chopped
   green onion for garnish

Mix all ingredients together, garnish and serve with tortilla chips.

Shrimp Dill Dip

Makes: 1½ c

8 oz pkg cream cheese
½ c yogurt
1 T fresh squeezed lemon or
   lime juice
½ tsp Tabasco
1 small clove garlic (crushed)
3 T green onion (chopped fine)

½ tsp Dijon-style mustard
½ tsp dill
½ tsp Worcestershire sauce
4½ oz shrimp (cooked and
   chopped), may use canned
salt and pepper to taste

In a covered container, cream together mayonnaise and cream cheese until blended and smooth. Add remaining ingredients and mix well. Refrigerate until ready for use. Great on wafers, raw vegetables, in sandwiches or on sliced French bread baguettes.

Herb Curry Dip

Makes: 1³/₄ c

1 c mayonnaise or salad dressing
½ c sour cream
1 tsp Fine Herbs (crushed)
¼ tsp salt
⅛ tsp curry powder

1 T parsley (snipped)
1 T onion (grated)
1½ tsp lemon juice
½ tsp Worcestershire sauce
2 tsp capers (drained)

In a covered container, mix all ingredients and store refrigerated until ready for use. This dip is wonderful with raw vegetables, prawns, thin slivers of cold roast lamb or beef.

Chutney Cheese Dip

Serves: 6-8

8 oz cream cheese
1 c Swiss cheese (grated)
1 T sherry
¼ tsp Lawry's seasoning salt
1 tsp curry powder
1 clove garlic (crushed)

¼ c walnuts (chopped)
1 green onion (chopped)
1 tsp parsley (chopped)
2-3 T chutney (regular or Hot & Spicey)

Blend cream cheese and Swiss cheese together. Add remaining ingredients (except chutney) and place into a covered container. Top with chutney and garnish with grated egg, parsley or orange rind. Serve as a spread with crackers or sliced cocktail breads.

Deviled Ham Dip

Makes: 2 c

2 (4¼ oz) cans deviled ham
1 (8 oz) pkg cream cheese
    (softened)
1 T chili powder
1 medium green onion (chopped)
1 T dry parsley or chervil

2 T pimiento (chopped)
1 tsp vinegar
½ tsp white wine or regular
Worcestershire sauce
pepper to taste
¼ tsp saffron (optional)

In a covered container, combine all ingredients and chill until service. Great on stone ground or sesame wafers.

Radish Dip

Makes: 3 c

1 c Ricotta cheese
2 c cottage cheese
¼ c carrot (grated)
¼ c green onion (chopped)
¼ c red radishes or dikon
    (chopped)
½ tsp basil

½ tsp oregano
1 T white wine Worcestershire
    sauce
½ tsp prepared horseradish
½ tsp salt
¼ tsp pepper
2 dashes Tabasco sauce

Combine all ingredients in a covered bowl and refrigerate until service. Serve with baguettes or raw vegetables.

Variation: Use for salad dressing by combining Ricotta and cottage cheese in blender or food processor until smooth. Add remaining ingredients and toss into a salad. Adjust herbs to taste.

SOUPS

Ginger Tomato Soup

Serves: 4

4 green onions (chopped)
½ cube butter or margarine
1 tomato (chopped)
1 T fresh ginger (grated)
1 (8 oz) can tomato sauce
1 can chicken stock or consommé

1 tsp white pepper
1 tsp salt
⅔ c white wine
pinch of sugar
½ c heavy cream

Sauté onion in butter until tender. Add tomato and cook until tomato is soft. Add remaining ingredients except cream, reduce heat and simmer for an additional 30 minutes. Add cream and simmer an additional 3-5 minutes. Place in a preheated thermos and serve hot at gametime with oyster crackers as garnish.

Lobster Shrimp Bisque

Serves: 8

2 c potatoes (diced)
1 c celery (coarse chopped)
½ c green onion (chopped)
½ cube butter or margarine
½ c dry sherry or vermouth
1 c fresh mushrooms (chopped fine)
2 c heavy cream
4 c milk
1½ tsp salt

¾ tsp pepper
½ c water
3 T cornstarch
4 T parsley (chopped fine)
½ lb lobster (cut into bite-size pieces)
½ lb baby shrimp
1 thinly sliced lemon or lime for garnish

In a large kettle, sauté potatoes, celery and onion in butter until tender. Add remaining ingredients, except cornstarch and water. Simmer about 1 hour, stirring occasionally. Dissolve cornstarch in water and add to chowder. Continue to cook an additional 15-20 minutes. Serve garnished with lemon slices. This is sheer elegance for a gourmet tailgate.

Orange and Gold Bisque

Serves: 8

1 cube butter or margarine
3 T flour
1 can evaporated milk
2½ c milk
1½ c chicken stock
4 medium carrots (grated)
¼ c green onion (chopped)

½ lb Cheddar cheese (grated)
½ c watercress or parsley
  (chopped)
2 tsp salt
1 tsp pepper
Tabasco sauce to taste

In a large saucepan, melt butter over medium heat. Using a wire whip add flour, milk and stock. Bring to a boil, lower heat and continue stirring until thickened. Add carrots and onion, cooking an additional 4-5 minutes. Blend cheese into mixture until melted. Add remaining ingredients and serve hot as a pregame warm-up with crusty French bread.

Blender Cream of Watercress Soup

Serves: 4-6

1 can evaporated milk
1 c milk
¾ c butter or margarine (softened)
¼ c flour
juice of 1 lemon
1 tsp pepper
1½ tsp celery salt

2 bunches watercress (cleaned
  and stemmed)
1 c chicken stock
2 T parsley (chopped)
1 T white wine Worcestershire
  sauce

Put all ingredients in blender and blend for 30 seconds. In a saucepan, heat soup over medium heat for about 15 minutes, stirring frequently. May be garnished with croutons, a sprig of watercress or a lemon slice. Elegant, light and easy.

Variations:
1. Substitute 1 bunch spinach for watercress.
2. Substitute 1 c chopped broccoli for watercress.

Borsch: The Beet-Um Soup

Serves: 3-4

2 T butter
1 carrot (diced)
1 onion (chopped)
5-6 beets with tops (chopped fine)
2 c beef stock or 1 can beef
    consommé
1 potato (diced)
1 T parsley (chopped)

½ bell pepper (chopped)
juice of 1 lemon
1 tsp salt
½ tsp pepper
1 bay leaf
1 tsp marjoram
½ c sour cream
horseradish on side

In a skillet, lightly sauté carrot and onion in butter. Add remaining ingredients (except sour cream). Bring to a boil then reduce heat and simmer covered 20 minutes. Pour into a preheated thermos and serve hot at game time with a dollop of sour cream. This is a good WARM UP or appetite teaser when you're serving lamb or beef.

Midwestern Corn Chowder

Serves: 6-8

¼ lb ham (cubed)
½ c water
2 T vermouth
2 dashes Worcestershire sauce
1 (10 oz) pkg frozen whole kernel
  corn
1 clove garlic (crushed)
1 medium onion (chopped)
1 large potato (peeled and
  chopped)

½ c red or green bell pepper
  (chopped fine)
1 (10½ oz) can condensed cream
  of mushroom soup
2 c milk
1 (16 oz) can cream-style corn
salt and pepper to taste
3 T fresh or 1 T dried parsley
  (chopped)

In a large saucepan, add ham, water, vermouth, Worcestershire, whole kernel corn, garlic, onion, potato and bell pepper. Cover and simmer over medium heat for 25-30 minutes or until potatoes are tender. Add condensed soup, milk, cream-style corn and parsley. Adjust salt and pepper to taste and continue heating an additional 10 minutes or until heated throughout. Pour into a preheated thermos and serve hot at gametime. Good served with hot French bread and butter.

Portuguese Mustard Green Soup

Serves: 6-8

1 c lima beans or horse beans
1 soup bone
1 tsp salt
1 tsp pepper
1 large onion (chopped)
2 medium potatoes (diced)

1 turnip (peeled and chopped)
½ bunch mustard greens
  (cleaned and chopped)

In a medium saucepan, cover

beans with water and cook for approximately 40 minutes over medium heat. Meanwhile, in a large pot, boil soup bone in 2½ quarts of water for 1 hour. Cool and drain beans, then blend in a blender. Add bean mixture blend in a blender. Add bean mixture and remaining ingredients to soup bone and continue cooking on low to medium heat for 2 hours. Correct seasonings and garnish with fresh mint.

Thermos Oyster Bisque

Serves: 6

1 pint oysters
2½ c milk
⅓ cube butter or margarine
½ c heavy cream
1 T cornstarch dissolved in ¼ c
   water

1 small onion (chopped fine)
1 egg (slightly beaten)
2 dashes Tabasco
3 T vermouth
2 T parsley (chopped)
salt and pepper to taste

In a saucepan, cook oysters in their liquid about 3-4 minutes. Drain and reserve liquid. Cut oysters into small pieces. Melt butter in a saucepan and add oyster liquid and cornstarch mixture. Wire whip constantly until thickened. Add remaining ingredients and simmer about ½ hour, stirring occasionally. Put soup into a heated thermos and serve hot at game in mugs or bowls with crackers or French bread. Can be used as an entrée or a hearty pregame warm-up.

Cabbage Soup

Serves: 8

4 c potatoes (chopped)
1 ham hock
3½ qts water
2 lbs cabbage (sliced)
1½ tsp pepper
2 T cilantro (chopped)
2 bay leaves
2 tsp basil

1 tsp dill
3 cloves garlic (crushed)
2 onions (chopped)
3 carrots (cut diagonally)
3 stalks celery (cut diagonally)
¼ lb fresh mushrooms (sliced)
½ c almonds (chopped or slivered)
¼ c green olives (chopped)

In a large pot, bring potatoes, ham hock and water to a boil. Reduce heat and add remaining ingredients. Simmer covered about 2 hours. Remove ham hock and pull off meat. Chop meat fine and return to soup. Correct seasonings. Serve hot at gametime with French cheese toast.

French Cheese Toast: Slice 1 loaf of French bread lengthwise and spread with Dijon-style mustard. Sprinkle with grated cheese of your choice and parsley. Put bread halves together and wrap in foil. Bake in a 325 degree oven until hot and bubbly. Wrap hot loaves and serve at gametime with soup.

50

SALADS
AND DRESSINGS

Artichoke Potato Tailgate Salad

Serves: 8

9-10 medium new potatoes
(cooked, peeled and sliced)
½ c red onion (chopped)
½ c celery (chopped)
7 hard boiled eggs (chopped)
2 tsp curry powder
1 c plain yogurt
½ c mayonnaise
½ c Dijon-style mustard

2-3 T vinegar
1 (6 oz) jar marinated artichoke
hearts (drained and sliced)
½ c green or red bell pepper
(chopped)
½ tsp tarragon
½ tsp dill weed
½ tsp celery salt
salt and pepper to taste

In a covered container, mix all ingredients together and chill until service. This salad may be served alone or on a bed of spinach leaves.

Salmon Pasta Salad

Serves: 6

1 can (7 oz) salmon
1 c frozen peas
2 hard boiled eggs (chopped)
1 small red onion (chopped fine)
½ c bell pepper (chopped)
½ c fresh mushrooms (chopped)
2 c shell macaroni (cooked)

½ tsp garlic powder
¼ tsp curry
¼ c Dijon-style mustard
4 oz sour cream
⅛ tsp cayenne pepper
1 c Fontina cheese (grated)
salt and pepper to taste

Combine all ingredients and refrigerate until service. May be served alone, on a bed of lettuce or used to stuff a tomato. To stuff tomatoes: Core 6 tomatoes and cut into sixths, cutting almost through. Fill with salmon mixture. Garnish with olives and green onion.

Gaspacho Salad Mold

Serves: 4-6

2 envelopes unflavored gelatin
²/₃ c beef broth
2 c tomato juice
2 tsp prepared horseradish
2 T lemon or lime juice
4 tsp Worcestershire sauce
1 c tomato (chopped)

1 c bell pepper (chopped)
1 c cucumber (chopped)
1 c zucchini (chopped)
½ c onion (finely chopped)
¼ c fresh cilantro (chopped)
3-4 cloves garlic (minced)

In a saucepan, soften gelatin in beef broth and heat over low heat until gelatin is dissolved. In a mixing bowl, combine gelatin mixture, tomato juice, horseradish, lemon juice and Worcestershire sauce. Chill till thickened. Blend in tomato, bell pepper, cucumber, zucchini, onion, cilantro and garlic. Pour into a mold and refrigerate until firm (4-6 hours). For service, unmold onto a lettuce-lined platter.

Japanese Vegetable Pickles

Makes: 4-6 c

½ small head cabbage (cored and cut into bite-size pieces)
½ head cauliflower (flowerettes only)
4 carrots (cut into sticks)
1 stalk celery (cut diagonally)

Brine
4 c water
2 c white vinegar
2 T salt
2 cloves garlic
½ tsp sugar
½ c parsley (chopped)
2 T soy sauce
2 T oyster sauce
1 T fresh ginger (grated)

Put washed and cut vegetables into a covered container and add brine. Cover and let sit out at room temperature for at least 1 day, then refrigerate an additional 2-3 days. This Japanese vinegary/salty salad can be served individually in very small amounts or as an appetizer on a large tray, eaten with chop sticks or fingers, depending on your dexterity.

Layered Taco Salad

Serves: 6-8

1 lb ground beef
1 (7 oz) can green chili salsa
2 T chili powder
2 cloves garlic (crushed)
salt and pepper to taste
3-4 medium tomatoes (chopped)
1 can medium pitted olives
1 small bunch green onions (chopped)
¼ lb fresh mushrooms (sliced)

1-2 heads lettuce (torn into bite-size pieces)
16 oz carton sour cream or plain unflavored yogurt
fresh or prepared Mexican salsa
½ lb Cheddar or Monterey Jack cheese (grated)
1 (16 oz) bag tortilla chips
1-2 avocados (slice at gametime)

In a skillet, brown meat with chili salsa, chili powder, garlic, salt and pepper. Simmer 5-10 minutes, drain and set aside to cool.

In a clear salad bowl, layer salad as follows: meat mixture, tomatoes, olives, green onions, mushrooms, lettuce and sour cream (make a well in sour cream and spoon in salsa, then encircle with grated cheese). At gametime serve with tortilla chips and avocado slices. This salad can be prepared up to 12 hours in advance and refrigerated until service.

Island Ginger Shrimp with Rice

Serves: 8

¼ tsp salt
½ tsp dry mustard
¼ tsp ground red peppers
¼ tsp curry
1 T horseradish
1 T fresh ginger (grated)
2 T capers (chopped)
1 can pineapple chunks
1 lb salad shrimp
1 medium bell pepper (chopped)

6 stalks celery (chopped)
½ can black olives (chop and
    retain remainder for garnish)
1 (2 oz) jar pimientos (chopped)
1 tsp parsley or cilantro
1 tsp green onions or chives
    (chopped)
6 c cooked rice
1-2 tomatoes (cut into wedges)

Combine all ingredients in a covered container. Mix thoroughly and refrigerate. Garnish with tomato wedges and remaining olives.

May be used for individual salads served on a bed of leaf lettuce.

Dublin Potato Salad

Serves: 7-8

1 tsp celery seed
1 T regular or malt vinegar
3 c potatoes (cooked and diced)
1 tsp dry mustard
2 tsp sugar
½ tsp salt
12 oz cooked or canned corned
    beef (chilled and diced)

2 c green or red cabbage
    (finely shredded)
¼ c dill pickle (chopped)
½ c green onion (chopped)
¾ c mayonnaise
2 T milk
½ tsp salt
pepper to taste

Soak celery seeds in vinegar for about 10 minutes. Drizzle over warm potatoes. Sprinkle with mustard, sugar and salt, then chill. Add remaining ingredients, toss lightly and keep refrigerated until gametime. This is a nice variation on potato salad.

Spinach/Garbanzo Pasta Salad   Serves: 6-8

12 oz twistee or Fusilli Pasta
1 red or green bell pepper
(julienne cut)
1 can (8 oz) garbanzo beans
(drained)
¼ c parsley (chopped)
½ c kidney beans (drained)
½ c yogurt
½ c red onion (chopped)
½ c mushrooms (chopped)

¼ c carrots (julienne)
1 tsp white wine Worcestershire
sauce
1 clove garlic (crushed)
1 tsp Lawry's seasoning salt
½ tsp savory
salt and pepper to taste
1 bunch spinach for liner
(washed and patted dry)

Cook twistee pasta in boiling water until tender. Drain and cool. Mix pasta with remaining ingredients (except spinach) and refrigerate until service. Serve pasta in a bowl or individually on spinach-lined plates.

Fruit and Yogurt Salad   Serves: 10

2 oranges (peeled and chunked)
½ pineapple (peeled and
chunked)
2 bananas (peeled and chunked)
½ c coconut (grated)
1-2 baskets strawberries (cleaned
and stemmed)

½ lb grapes (cleaned and
stemmed)
2 apples (cored and chunked)
2 tsp lemon or lime juice
1 (8 oz) container vanilla yogurt
3 dashes cinnamon

Mix all ingredients and refrigerate in covered container until service. Serve with a sprig of mint.

Variations: Substitute ½ tsp almond extract for cinnamon. Or sprinkle with granola or 1 c chopped nuts.

Tabuli Salad

1 cup bulgur
1 cup boiling water
1 1/4 c oil
1 1/4 c lemon juice
salt and pepper
1/4 bunch parsley
1/2 bell pepper (chopped)
2 oz jar pimientos (chopped)

2 T mint (fresh) (optional)
1/2 c grated onion
1/2 c celery (chopped)
1-2 fresh tomatoes (chopped)
1/4 c white vinegar
1/2 c whole olives
2-3 cloves garlic (crushed)

Pour boiling water over bulgur and let double. Add remaining ingredients and refrigerate at least 4 hours before serving. We like to make it a day ahead of time to really let the flavors mingle, otherwise it tastes a little grainy.

Smoked Salmon Salad

Serves: 6

6 medium-sized new potatoes
  (cooked and cooled)
3 hard boiled eggs (chopped)
1/4 lb smoked salmon (cut into
  chunks)
1/2 c onion (chopped)
1 1/2 tsp capers

1 tsp dill weed
1 tsp pepper
1/4 c rice wine vinegar
1 T lemon or lime juice
1/4 c olive oil
1 T chervil or parsley (minced)
1 T pimiento

In a large mixing bowl, cut potatoes into bite-size pieces. Add eggs and salmon. In a separate bowl, blend remaining ingredients and add to salmon mixture. Refrigerate and let stand at least 2 hours. Serve alone or on a bed of lettuce leaves. Garnish with fresh dill, parsley or lemon.

Cold Pasta Salad

8 oz fettucine noodles (cooked and drained)
1 c broccoli flowerettes (chopped)
½ c carrot (grated)
½ c red or green onion (chopped fine)
¼ c tarragon vinegar

½ c mayonnaise
½ c Parmesan cheese (grated)
1 tsp tarragon
1 tsp salt
1 tsp pepper
1 tsp dill

Mix all ingredients together and refrigerate in a covered container at least 1-2 hours or overnight. May be made up to 2 days ahead of time. Keep chilled until service and use as an interesting alternative to macaroni or potato salad.

Italian Potato Salad

4 c cooked potatoes (diced)
3 c zucchini (chopped)
½ lb fresh mushrooms (sliced)
1 tomato (chopped)
⅛ lb dry salami (julienne sliced)
3-4 wax peppers (sliced)
½ c olive oil

1½ T lemon or lime juice
⅓ c vinegar
1 small red onion (chopped)
1 T Italian seasoning
2 cloves garlic (crushed)
salt and pepper to taste

Place potatoes, zucchini, mushrooms, tomato, salami and wax peppers into a large covered bowl. Mix together remaining ingredients and pour over vegetables. Carefully blend salad without breaking potatoes and refrigerate until service. This is a very unusual potato salad that works well with barbecue meat.

Carrot/Grape Slaw

Serves: 6

Dressing
1/2 c sour cream or plain yogurt
1 tsp prepared horseradish
3 T mayonnaise
1 tsp lemon or vinegar
1/4 tsp salt
3 dashes pepper

Salad
2 c carrots (grated)
1 c seedless grapes (Thompson
    or Red Flame are good)
1/2 c celery (chopped fine)
1/4 c bell pepper (chopped fine)
1/4 c apple (chopped fine)
1/4 c almonds (sliced)

Combine all ingredients for dressing, cover and refrigerate until ready to make salad. This is something you could make ahead.

Prepare vegetables and fruit and place in a covered bowl. Blend in dressing and refrigerate for at least 1 hour before serving.

Variations:

1. Substitute raisins, currants or other fresh fruit for grapes in this recipe. Or add napa cabbage.

2. Substitute head cabbage for carrots or 2 sliced bananas in place of the grapes. Omit the bell pepper for this substitution.

Maui Chicken Salad

Serves: 8

1 lb chicken breast (skinned)
1/2 medium onion (chopped)
1 c celery (chopped)
1 (4 oz) can water chestnuts
    (sliced)
1 c cooked rice
1 c fresh or canned pineapple
    tidbits

1 c shredded coconut
1/2 c bell pepper (chopped)
3/4 c mayonnaise
1/4 c sour cream
1 tsp curry
1 T fresh squeezed lemon juice
salt and pepper to taste

In a saucepan, cover chicken with water and simmer approximately 20-30 minutes or until done. Drain, cool and shred chicken. In a covered container, add remaining ingredients and mix well. Chill until service.

May be served over chinese cabbage or lettuce. Easy garnish would be slivered almonds, radishes, toasted sesame seeds or grated carrot. This is a cool, fabulous summertime addition to barbecue ribs, steak, shrimp or chicken.

Artichoke Salad

Serves: 8

1 c olive oil
½ c cider vinegar
1 (2 oz) jar pimientos
2 hard boiled eggs (grated)
1 bunch green onions (chopped)

1 large jar artichoke hearts
    (undrained)
2 T capers
1 tsp bell pepper (chopped)
2-3 heads of butter or leaf lettuce

In a covered bowl, mix oil and vinegar vigorously with a wire whip. Add rest of ingredients and refrigerate for at least 6 hours. To serve, tear lettuce into bite-sized pieces and arrange on plates or in a large bowl. Top with artichoke mixture. We like this salad because it can be made up ahead of time and then served at YOUR leisure. Artichoke mixture can be refrigerated up to 4 days.

Pazazz Potato Salad

Serves: 8

3 lbs potatoes (cooked and peeled)
½ c vegetable oil
¼ c tarragon vinegar
¼ c chicken consommé
¼ c green onions (chopped)
½ c bell pepper (chopped)

2 T parsley (chopped)
½ tsp tarragon (dried)
½ tsp dill
1 clove garlic (crushed)
salt and pepper to taste

Cube potatoes, combine with other ingredients and toss gently. Cover and refrigerate until service. This salad also looks very nice served on individual plates of chopped or leaf lettuce.

Steamy Winter Potato Salad

Serves: 8

6-7 slices bacon
bacon drippings
1 ½ T flour
1 c beef bouillon
⅓ c vinegar
pepper to taste
1 T sugar

6 medium potatoes (cooked and
   peeled)
2 stalks celery (sliced)
1 cucumber (peeled and sliced)
2 green onions (chopped)
½ small head red cabbage
   (chopped)

In a skillet, cook bacon until crisp. Remove, drain and crumble. Heat bacon drippings, add flour and cook over medium heat for 3 minutes. Stirring constantly, add beef bouillon, and cook until thickened. Blend in vinegar, pepper and sugar. Remove from heat.

Slice potatoes. In a covered casserole, alternate layers of potato, celery, cucumber, onion, bacon crumbs and cabbage. Pour vinegar mixture over vegetables and heat slowly at about 300 degrees for 45-50 minutes. For service, toss everything together without breaking potatoes. Serve hot at gametime. May be garnished with sliced radishes or snipped chives.

Crab Salad

Serves: 8

2 c crab (cooked and flaked)
1 c celery (diced)
2 cloves garlic (crushed)
2 hard boiled eggs (chopped)
1 green onion (chopped)
2 dashes cayenne
½ tsp dill weed

salt and pepper
1 T olive or vegetable oil
1 T vinegar
2 lemons (cut into wedges)
4 avocados (halved and dipped in
   lemon juice)

In a covered bowl, mix all ingredients except lemons and avocados. Mound crab mixture on lettuce in a salad bowl topped with avocado slices or serve individual salad of avocado halves and crab. May be garnished with lemon, cilantro, watercress, pimiento or lemon mint.

Variation: Substitute cooked and flaked salmon, lobster or shrimp in place of crab.

Tostada Chicken Salad
Serves: 8 (It grows)

1 bag tortilla chips
1 (16 oz) can refried beans
2 whole chickens (boiled and meat shredded)
1 head lettuce (chopped)
1 bunch green onions (chopped)
4 tomatoes (chopped)
1 bunch cilantro (optional)
8 oz Cheddar cheese (grated)
2-3 mashed avocados (with 2 T lemon juice added)
1 can pitted black olives
16 oz sour cream
1 small can jalapeño peppers (retain juice for dressing)
** these peppers are HOT

Dressing
³/₄ c vinegar
¹/₂ c oil
2 cloves garlic (crushed)
¹/₂ tsp oregano
¹/₂ tsp sugar
¹/₄ tsp dry mustard
¹/₂ tsp paprika
salt and pepper to taste
jalapeño pepper juice to taste

Mix all ingredients for dressing and store in a covered container. This is an entertaining salad as it is done self service-style. Have everything out in order of service and let your guests do the work. This is a fine entrée salad for warm afternoon games. Assemble as follows:

tortilla chips
beans (served hot or cold)
shredded chicken
lettuce
tomatoes
onions
mashed avocado

salad dressing
cheese
sour cream
olives
cilantro and a jalapeño pepper
    to garnish

Marinated Prawns

4-5 green onions (chopped)
½ tsp cayenne pepper
1 tsp salt
½ tsp white pepper
¼ c olive oil

1 c lemon or lime juice
3 T fresh cilantro (chopped)
½ c chili sauce
1 T capers
1½ lbs steamed prawns

Mix all ingredients together and refrigerate in a covered container for at least two hours. May be served with cocktail sauce and crackers on the side or as a seafood salad on lettuce.

Variation: Use to marinate raw, skinned and deboned fresh fish.

Moch Caesar Salad Dressing

Makes: 1½ c

juice of 1 whole lemon
1 tsp Worcestershire sauce
¼ tsp pepper (ground or cayenne)
¼ tsp dry mustard
2 egg yolks
4 cloves garlic (crushed)
1 (2 oz) can anchovies (minced)

½ c olive oil
2 heads romaine lettuce (torn into
   pieces)
Parmesan cheese
seasoned croutons
fresh ground pepper

In a food processor or blender, combine first 7 ingredients and refrigerate. Toss with bite-size romaine lettuce, seasoned croutons, Parmesan cheese and fresh ground pepper to taste. (We tend to like a lot of Parmesan as it smells and tastes good.)

Seasoned croutons are available at most grocery stores or can be made at home. This salad is always terribly elegant for a tailgate and tastes wonderful.

Crumbled Blue Cheese Dressing

Makes: 2 c

1 c vinegar
½ c olive or vegetable oil
½ tsp paprika
½ tsp dry mustard
½ tsp garlic powder

½ tsp sugar
½ tsp salt
dash of pepper
4 oz Blue cheese (crumbled)

In a cruet or covered container, shake or whip all ingredients together and refrigerate until use. This is one of my favorite dressings because it has the lighter oil and vinegar base but all the rich taste of blue cheese. I tend to put more vinegar than oil because of calories, but adjust to your taste and consistency.

Green Salad with Mixed Nut Dressing

Makes: 1¼ c

½ c raw cashews
2 T unsalted sunflower seeds
1 T sesame seeds
6-8 almonds
1 c sesame oil
1 clove garlic (crushed)
1 T vinegar

3 T lime or lemon juice
½ tsp Dijon-style mustard
½ tsp basil
½ tsp thyme
¼ tsp parsley
salt and pepper to taste

In a baking pan, lightly toast nuts in a 350 degree oven. Spread them out and bake 10-15 minutes, stirring frequently until golden. Remove from heat and cool. Using a food processor or blender, grind nuts and garlic almost to a powder. Add vinegar, lemon juice, mustard and herbs. Mix in thoroughly. With motor on, slowly pour in oil until completely blended. Store in a covered container, refrigerate until ready for use. For service, use as an unusual new idea on leaf lettuce or spinach.

Curry Dill Salad Dressing

Makes: 2½ c

½ c wine vinegar
1½ tsp salt
1½ tsp pepper
1½ T dill

1 tsp curry
3 T mayonnaise
½ tsp mustard
½ c olive oil or vegetable oil

In food processor or blender, mix all ingredients but oil. While processor is running gradually add oil until it is thoroughly incorporated. Put dressing into a shaker bottle and refrigerate until ready for use. Excellent on green or spinach salad.

Chutney Spinach Dressing

Makes: 1½ c

½ c chutney
⅓ c herb vinegar
¼-½ tsp fresh grated ginger
1 green onion (chopped fine)

½ c oil
½ tsp dry mustard
1 clove garlic (crushed)

Blend all ingredients and store in a covered container in refrigerator until use. This is an easy and different variation to the normal spinach salad dressings. Garnish salad with sliced fresh mushrooms, shrimp and chopped egg.

Bayou Blue Cheese Dressing

Makes: 4 c

8 oz blue cheese (crumbled)
2 c plain yogurt
1 c mayonnaise
½ c buttermilk
3 T onion (finely chopped)
4 cloves garlic (crushed)
¼ c lemon juice

2 T Dijon-style mustard
1 T celery (minced)
1 tsp ginger
dash of Tabasco
2 T Worcestershire sauce
2 T capers (chopped)

Blend all ingredients together in a covered container and refrigerate until service.

Chinese Salad Dressing

Makes: 1½ c

¾ c vinegar or lemon juice
¾ c soy sauce
3 T sugar
1 T fresh ginger (grated)

1 clove garlic (minced)
¼ tsp hot mustard
2 T sherry
¼ c salad oil

In a container, mix all ingredients but oil until thoroughly blended. Gradually add salad oil, stirring constantly. Store in covered container. This dressing can be used with cucumbers, mushrooms, tomatoes, Chinese cabbage, lettuce or even leftover bits of meat.
  *For LO Calorie: omit oil.

Snowshoe Spinach Dressing

¼ c sugar (or less to taste)
1 tsp salt
½ tsp dill
1 tsp dry mustard
1 T onion (minced)

1 T parsley (chopped fine)
3 T vermouth
1 c oil
½ c low fat cottage cheese

Blend spices, vermouth and oil in bowl. With wire whip, mix in cottage cheese and whip together. Store in covered container in refrigerator.

Toss dressing with washed and chopped fresh spinach. Garnish with hard boiled egg, bacon, mushrooms, cheese, tomato, etc. Or any combination of these items. It's your salad — improvise!

BARBECUE

Steak Pinwheels
with Flavored Butters

Serves: 6-8

3-4 lbs flank or round steak
salt and pepper
thyme, marjoram, crushed bay leaf, garlic powder
flavored butters (recipes follow)

Have butcher run steak through tenderizer or score meat against the grain at home. Spread butter or filling evenly on one side of meat. Roll steak lengthwise, salt, pepper and spice exterior. Slice into 1-2 inch pinwheels. Secure rolls with a skewer. Barbecue steaks about 5-10 minutes on each side, or as desired.

Flavored Butters

Garlic Butter
½ c butter (softened)
1-3 cloves garlic (peeled and
    crushed)
1 tsp parsley (chopped fine)

Anchovy or Smoked Oyster Butter
½ c butter or margarine
    (softened)
½-1 tsp anchovy paste or
    3-4 smoked oysters (mashed)
¼ tsp onion (grated)
½ tsp lemon juice
1 garlic clove (crushed)

Herb Butter
½ c butter or margarine
    (softened)
2 tsp parsley (chopped fine)
2 tsp prepared Dijon-style
    mustard
1 tsp Worcestershire sauce
2 cloves garlic (crushed)
1 tsp oregano
1 tsp basil
1 T onion (chopped fine)
salt and pepper to taste

Mix ingredients together by hand or in a food processor until thoroughly incorporated. Refrigerate and store in a covered container for use.

Variation: Add 1-2 large sliced mushrooms.

Ginger/Soy Chicken

Serves: 6

5 lbs chicken (quartered)
3 T white wine
1/2 c soy sauce
3 T brown sugar or molasses
1/4 tsp curry powder
1 T sherry

2 T brandy
1 T fresh ginger root (grated)
1 clove garlic (crushed)
1 green onion (chopped)
1 orange squeezed or 2 T orange
    juice concentrate

Precook chicken pieces for 20 minutes in a 325 degree oven. Mix remaining ingredients, marinate and refrigerate chicken until ready for barbecue. Barbecue 15 to 20 minutes to desired doneness. Use extra marinade to baste.

Shish Kebob

Serves: 6

3/4 c wine vinegar
1/4 c soy sauce
1/2 c red wine
2 cloves garlic (crushed)
2 bay leaves (crushed)
1 lb lamb shoulder or beef steak
    (cut into 1 inch cubes)
black pepper to taste

1 T Grenadine
3 tomatoes (cut into wedges) or
    1 basket cherry tomatoes
18 medium mushrooms
3 small onions (cut into sixths)
6 slices bacon (cut into thirds)
1-2 bell peppers (cut into 18 large
    pieces)

In a covered container, combine vinegar, soy sauce, wine, garlic and bay leaves. Rub meat with pepper and Grenadine and add to marinade. Marinate meat for 6 hours or overnight.

Remove meat from marinade and arrange meat, tomatoes, mushrooms, onion, bacon and bell pepper on skewers. Refrigerate until ready to barbecue. Barbecue 8-10 minutes, or as desired. Use leftover marinade to baste. Can be served as is or in French rolls as a sandwich.

Variation: Add to marinade 1 tsp curry powder, 1 tsp ginger or 1 T chili powder.

Lemon Marinated Ribs

3-4 lbs ribs
1 onion (chopped fine)
juice of 3 lemons
¼ c dry white wine
½ c wine vinegar
½ tsp basil

¼ tsp thyme
½ tsp chili powder
1 T Worcestershire sauce
2 cloves garlic (crushed)
1 tsp prepared horseradish

Day Before: Wipe ribs with a damp cloth to remove bone fragments etc. Precook ribs in a shallow pan for 1 hour at 325 degrees or microwave 15-20 minutes. Move ribs to a covered container. Mix other ingredients and use to marinate ribs overnight.

Game Day: Refrigerate until ready to use, barbecue as desired, using extra marinade to baste.

This marinade is a nice change from the tomato-based marinades and sauces.

Stuffed Whole Barbecued Fish

4-5 lbs whole tuna, salmon, cod
   or red snapper
salt and pepper
garlic powder
1 c zucchini (cut julienne)
1 onion (thinly sliced)
2 plum tomatoes (chopped) or
   1/3 c tomato sauce
1/2 c celery (cut julienne)
1 bell pepper (diced) or pimiento
2 carrots (cut julienne)

1 T parsley (chopped)
1 (5 oz) can water chestnuts
   (drained and chopped)
3 T soy sauce
2 T oyster sauce
1 T fresh ginger (grated)
2 bay leaves (crumbled)
1/4 tsp thyme
1/2 tsp basil
juice of 2 lemons

Take clean, gutted fish and gently press open body cavity. Sprinkle inside and outside of fish with salt, pepper and garlic powder. Mix remaining ingredients and fill cavity with mixture. Close with string, heavy thread or skewers. Wrap fish securely in foil and barbecue both sides (approximately 25-30 minutes total or until flesh flakes easily).

Variations:
1. We have grape vines in the yard so we wrap the fish in 1-2 layers of grape leaves and then foil. I like a bit of fresh dill in my vegetable mixture.
2. Substitute 1/2 tsp Cajun spice for the oyster sauce.

Spicey Stuffed Pork Tenderloin   Serves: 6

Stuffing

1 red and green bell pepper
(seeded and chopped)
10-12 mushrooms (chopped)
½ c onion (chopped)
½ c celery (chopped)
2 T parsley (chopped)
1 bay leaf (crushed)
1 tsp thyme (crushed)

½ tsp cayenne pepper
1 clove garlic (crushed)
½ tsp salt
½ tsp chili powder
1 tsp white wine Worcestershire
  sauce
2 T oil

2 (1 lb) pieces pork tenderloin or 6 thick cut pork chops
1 c dry white wine
fennel seed

In a skillet, sauté all ingredients for stuffing until vegetables are tender. With a sharp knife, remove fat and membrane from meat. Cut tenderloins lengthwise almost to opposite side. Cover with plastic wrap and pound from center out until about ½ inch thick.

Spread vegetable mixture over the two pieces of pounded tenderloin to within ½ inch of the edge. Roll and secure with metal skewers. In a covered container sprinkle meat with wine and fennel. Refrigerate until gametime. Barbecue for about 1½ hours to desired doneness. Slice and serve with salad, French bread, etc. This is fabulous tasting, elegant and a nice break from steak.

Variation: For pork chops, slice chop lengthwise almost to form a pocket. Fill each chop with vegetable mixture and secure with metal skewer. Barbecue about 45 minutes to desired doneness.

Marinated Chuck Roast

Serves: 6-8

3-4 lbs chuck roast
4-5 garlic cloves (peeled and
  halved)
½ c red wine
½ c soy sauce

½ tsp Cajun seasoning
¼ c sugar
1 tsp nutmeg (or to taste)
½ tsp salt
juice of 1 orange

Make about 10 slits in roast and insert garlic halves. Mix marinade and marinate meat overnight in a covered container. Keep refrigerated until gametime and barbecue as desired. Use extra marinade to baste.

Barbecued Butterflied Leg of Lamb

Serves: 8-10

1 (6-7 lb) leg of lamb (have butcher
  butterfly)
3-4 cloves garlic (peeled and
  halved)
1 c Madiera
3 T olive oil

1 T tarragon
1 tsp dried mint
½ c soy sauce
1 (6 oz) can tomato sauce
½ tsp salt
½ tsp white pepper

Make 6-8 (1 inch) slits in lamb and insert garlic. Wire whip remaining ingredients and marinate lamb in a covered container overnight. Plan to barbecue lamb 1-1½ hours to desired doneness. Baste lamb every 20 minutes with extra marinade. Can be served alone or in sandwiches.

Variations:

Grenadine Leg of Lamb

6-7 lb butterflied leg of lamb
½ c Grenadine
salt and pepper
¼ c parsley (chopped)

2-3 cloves garlic (crushed)
½ c onion (chopped fine)
½ c brandy

Rub lamb with salt, pepper, Grenadine, parsley and garlic. Sprinkle with onions and brandy. Cover and refrigerate overnight or until gametime. Barbecue lamb for 1-1½ hours until desired doneness. Baste with remaining marinade every 20 minutes.

Garlic Herb Leg of Lamb

6-7 lb butterflied leg of lamb
3 cloves garlic (crushed)
salt and pepper to taste
¾ c white wine
2 T butter or margarine
¼ tsp marjoram
½ tsp rosemary

¼ tsp thyme
½ tsp sage
juice of 1 lemon
1 T white wine Worcestershire
  sauce
1 T Parmesan cheese

Rub leg of lamb with salt and pepper and combine remaining ingredients. Marinate lamb in a covered container for at least 4-6 hours or overnight. Keep refrigerated until ready for barbecue then cook as desired.

Snapper with a Snap

Serves: 6-8

Excellent with steaks and fillets of snapper, bass, cod, albacore, tuna

2¹/₂-3 lbs red snapper fillets
¹/₄ tsp salt
¹/₂ c oil
3 T fresh ginger (grated)
¹/₂ c green onion (chopped)

¹/₄ c fresh cilantro (chopped) or
  2 T dried
¹/₂ c soy sauce
dash of cayenne or Tabasco
2 tsp parsley (chopped)

Mix all ingredients and pour over fish. Marinate at least 1-2 hours. Barbecue until fish flakes. Use extra marinade to baste.

Snappy Sauce
¹/₂ c sour cream
¹/₂ c fresh or prepared salsa

Wire whip together and refrigerate until service. Use to top fish and garnish with fresh cilantro.

Hot and Sweet Barbecued Ribs

Serves: 8

May be done on barbecue or in oven.

6-8 lbs spareribs
salt and pepper to taste
3 c water
¹/₂ c vinegar

1 tsp Tabasco sauce
3 c Hot and Sweet Barbecue sauce
  (see recipe below)

Rub ribs with salt and pepper and place in shallow baking pan. Mix water, vinegar and Tabasco and pour over ribs. Cover with tin foil and bake in a 325 degree oven for 1 hour.

Oven Method: Add barbecue sauce and bake an additional ½ hour at 350 degrees, basting periodically.

Barbecue Method: Take cold precooked ribs to game and grill on barbecue for 15-20 minutes. Generously baste ribs with Hot and Sweet Sauce.

Hot and Sweet Barbecue Sauce

½ c oyster sauce	2 tsp prepared mustard
2 c tomato sauce	4 cloves garlic (crushed)
½ c white wine	2 onions (finely chopped)
2 tsp oil	½ tsp chili powder or paste
2 tsp brown sugar	1 tsp crushed red pepper
1 tsp salt	cayenne pepper to taste

In a saucepan, mix ingredients and simmer onions till tender. Stir constantly. May be refrigerated for later use.

Amaretto Barbecued Chicken   Serves: 6-8

1 T butter or margarine	¼ c honey
1-2 green onions (chopped fine)	2 T white wine Worcestershire
½ c amaretto	sauce
½ c catsup	1 tsp Tabasco sauce
½ tsp prepared horseradish	1 chicken cut into pieces
¼ c white wine	

In a saucepan, sauté onions in butter until just tender. Add remaining ingredients (except chicken) and simmer for an additional minute or two. In a covered container, pour marinade over chicken and marinate overnight. (You may want to precook chicken at home in the oven or microwave for 15-20 minutes to help cut down on barbecue time.) Barbecue to doneness, reserving extra marinade and using it as a baste. This is a great marinade for boneless chicken breast if you just want to do barbecue chicken sandwiches. Serve with a green salad and bread.

Tailgate Chateaubriand

Serves: 4-6

1½ tsp salt
½ tsp pepper
½ tsp garlic powder or 1 clove
   garlic (crushed)
1 tsp Lawry's seasoning salt
1 pkg dry French or Italian
   dressing

1 c vegetable oil
½ c wine vinegar
3 T brandy or scotch
2-3 lbs chateaubriand or chuck
   roast

Mix marinade ingredients and pour over meat in a covered container. Marinate meat 4-6 hours or overnight before game. Barbecue meat as desired, using extra marinade for further basting. Meat may be served whole, thinly sliced for sandwiches, with bearnaise sauce, in tortillas, etc.

Skewered Shrimp
with Garlic and Basil

Serves: 6

18 raw prawns (peeled and
  deveined)
2-3 cloves garlic (crushed)
1 c white wine
¼ c olive oil (or vegetable oil)
1 tsp Worcestershire sauce
1 tsp basil
½ tsp oregano

½ tsp pepper
1 lemon (squeezed)
bamboo skewers
Optional: Clean, raw vegetables
  such as zucchini, onion, cherry
  tomatoes, bell pepper, lemon
  slices, carrot sticks, corn cob-
  bettes or celery.

In a covered container, combine first 9 ingredients and marinate at least 2-3 hours. Remove from marinade and skewer alone or with vegetables. Refrigerate until gametime. Grill until shrimp is pink and vegetables are tender. About 3-7 minutes. Use left over marinade to baste while barbecuing. Serve immediately.

*For denser vegetables like corn, partially cook by blanching or microwaving for a few minutes before skewering.

Barbecued Grilled
Blue Cheese Burgers

Serves: 4

1 lb lean ground beef
½ lb ground pork
2 oz crumbled blue cheese
½ tsp salt

¼ tsp pepper
½ tsp basil
½ tsp parsley (dried)

In a mixing bowl, combine all ingredients and mix well. Form into patties, wrap, and refrigerate until game time. Barbecue to desired doneness. Serve alone or with crisp bacon on buns.

Variation: Add 1 egg and 3 crumbled soda crackers to meat mixture. Roll into meatballs and use as an appetizer.

Fish Kebobs

Serves: 4-6

1½-2 lbs fresh halibut, etc. (cut into 1½ inch chunks)
½ lb fresh mushrooms (washed)
1 red pepper (cut into chunks)
2 medium zucchini (cut into 1 inch rounds)
4 pearl onions

Skewer ingredients and brush with Barbecue Sauce. Grill quickly, turning after 5-8 minutes.

Barbecue Sauce

3 T lemon or lime juice
1 T olive oil
1 T chives (chopped)
3 dashes white wine Worcestershire sauce

½ tsp saffron
1 tsp chervil
salt and pepper to taste

Option: See index for other marinade ideas.

Grilled Stuffed Chicken Breasts

Serves: 4

4 chicken breasts (halved,
   deboned, skinned)
¼ lb Fontina or Monterey Jack
   cheese
3-4 fresh mushrooms (chopped)

1 tsp basil
1 tsp fresh parsley (chopped fine)
½ tsp garlic powder
2 T melted butter or olive oil

Pound chicken breasts with meat mallet to ¼ inch thickness. Slice cheese into 4 pieces and place one in center of each breast. Sprinkle breasts with mushrooms, basil and parsley. Roll and secure with wooden skewers. Brush each breast with butter or oil and package until game time. Grill over medium coals for about 15-20 minutes. These are great topped with a sweet and sour, teriyaki, mustard or caper sauce. See index for recipes.

Louisiana Barbecued Shrimp

Serves: 4

1 1/2 lbs raw prawns (peeled and deveined)
3 T olive or vegetable oil
2 T prepared barbecue sauce
1 T Worcestershire sauce
1 T lemon juice
2 cloves garlic (crushed)
1 tsp parsley

3/4 tsp ground red pepper
3/4 tsp Liquid Smoke
1/2 tsp paprika
1/2 tsp oregano
1/4 tsp hot pepper or Tabasco sauce
salt and pepper to taste

Skewer shrimp, combine remaining ingredients, and pour over shrimp. Refrigerate overnight and spoon marinade over shrimp occasionally if possible. Barbecue prawns until done, using extra marinade to baste. These are excellent served with crusty French bread, corn on the cob and a salad.

California Barbecue Sauce

Makes: 3 c

1 T oil
1/3 c onion (chopped fine)
2 cloves garlic (crushed)
1 c tomato sauce
1/4 c vinegar
1 c red wine

1 T soy sauce
1 T dry mustard
1/4 c Worcestershire sauce
2 tsp Tabasco sauce
1 T chili powder
1 T brown sugar or honey

In a saucepan, sauté onions and garlic in oil until tender. Add remaining ingredients and simmer for another 1/2 hour. Stir occasionally. Keep in covered container until ready for use. This barbecue sauce is great for chicken, beef and pork, and try it for a change with barbecue fish.

Ginger Marinade

½ c soy sauce
¼ c honey or Karo syrup
1 clove garlic (crushed)
⅓ c sherry

1 T fresh ginger (grated)
1 T lemon juice
¼ tsp prepared horseradish

Combine all ingredients in a covered bowl and refrigerate until ready for use. Pour over meat and marinate at least 4-6 hours or overnight. Barbecue as desired, basting with remaining marinade. Meat prepared this way would be good served alone, sliced as an appetizer or used on a Chinese Salad (see salad section).

Beer Marinade for Chicken

1 cube butter or margarine
1 T sage
2 tsp oregano
1 bay leaf
½ tsp salt

¼ tsp pepper
1 T Worcestershire sauce
2-3 cloves garlic (crushed)
¼ tsp Tabasco sauce
1 can beer

One day before your tailgate: precook chicken by baking for 20 minutes at 325 degrees. Refrigerate until time to barbecue.

Game time: In a metal pan on barbecue, melt butter and add all ingredients except beer. Dredge precooked chicken in this butter mixture and start barbecuing. My dad likes this next part. Add ½ to 1 can of beer to remaining marinade and brush onto chicken as it cooks. (I'll leave it to you to decide what happens to the beer that doesn't make it into the marinade.) Keep chicken moving on grill. This marinade not only smells and tastes great but is an interesting alternative sauce.

Bird Marinade

Great with chicken, duck, pheasant or basketball**

½ c white wine Worcestershire
    sauce
½ c soy sauce
2 T vermouth
2 dashes Tabasco
2 T oyster sauce

2 T lemon or lime juice
¼ onion (chopped fine)
5 cloves garlic (crushed)
4 T parsley (chopped)
¼ tsp Cajun seasoning

Combine all ingredients in a covered bowl and add meat. Marinate for at least 3 hours or overnight. Keep refrigerated until ready for barbecue. Barbecue as desired, using extra marinade to baste.

Wine Marinade

Makes: 1½ c

For beef, pork or lamb.

½ c dry red or white wine
½ c catsup
½ tsp prepared horseradish
¼ c oil
3 T herb or wine vinegar
2 cloves garlic (crushed)

2 T onion (chopped fine)
1 T parsley (chopped)
1 T Worcestershire sauce
1 bay leaf
salt and pepper
2 tsp fresh or 1 tsp dry rosemary

Combine all ingredients and marinate meat for at least 3 hours or overnight. Refrigerate until ready to barbecue. Use extra marinade to baste meat while cooking.

Brandy Marinade

1 c oil
½ c brandy
½ c dry white wine
1 carrot (chopped)
2 T parsley (chopped)
½ tsp thyme

1 bay leaf (crumbled)
½ onion (chopped)
2 cloves garlic (crushed)
½ tsp tarragon
salt and pepper

Mix all ingredients and marinate meat for at least 3 hours or overnight. Keep refrigerated until gametime, then barbecue as desired, using extra marinade to baste.

Duck Marinade

1 domestic duck
pepper
1 clove garlic (crushed)
1 T Worcestershire sauce
¼ c sherry
½ c soy sauce

½ c white wine
1 small onion (peeled and
   quartered)
1 orange (peeled and sectioned)
¼ c apricot or plum preserves

Combine garlic, Worcestershire, sherry and soy sauce in a covered container. Add duck and marinate for 4-6 hours. Remove bird from marinade, place onion and orange into body cavity and skewer closed. Reserve marinade. Use part to baste duck during cooking. Bake or barbecue until almost to desired doneness. Add apricot preserves to reserved marinade and brush over duck. Continue cooking till done. (The preserves tend to darken when cooked and could cause the duck to burn if you're not careful.)

Note: If using wild duck, cooking times will vary with age. If you get a really old bird it may take all afternoon to cook it to doneness. When you are unsure of the age of the bird, give yourself plenty of time when cooking.

Venison Marinade

6-8 steaks, chops or a butterflied
   roast of venison or beef
¼ c beef consommé
½ c red wine
½ c soy sauce
⅓ c brandy or sherry

¼ c onion (chopped fine)
1 T lemon or lime juice
2 T honey or brown sugar
½ tsp black pepper
¼ tsp sage (crushed)
1 tsp garlic powder

Mix all ingredients and marinate meat overnight in refrigerator. Barbecue meat as desired. Use extra marinade to baste. This marinade would be appropriate for beef also.

CASSEROLES
AND SIDE DISHES

Clam Fettucine

Serves: 8

1 lb fettucine noodles
4 cloves garlic (minced)
½ cube butter or margarine
2 (6.5 oz) cans minced clams
3-4 dashes Worcestershire sauce
¼ c parsley (finely chopped)

½ tsp salt
¼ tsp white pepper
2 T onion (grated)
½ c heavy cream
1 tsp cornstarch
Parmesan cheese

Cook noodles in 6 qts boiling water until tender. Drain and run under cool water for a minute. Place in a warm casserole. In a saucepan, heat remaining ingredients except cornstarch and Parmesan cheese. Simmer about 25-30 minutes. Blend cornstarch into ¼ c cold water and add to clam sauce. Simmer until lightly thickened. Spoon over pasta, toss with Parmesan cheese and serve immediately.

Italian Stuffed Eggplant

Serves: 8

2 large eggplants (quartered
  lengthwise)
½ c olive or vegetable oil
¾ lb lean ground beef or Italian
sausage
2 cloves garlic (crushed)
1 bell pepper (chopped)
1 large onion (chopped)
1 tomato (diced)

¼ c fresh parsley or cilantro
  (chopped)
¼ tsp basil
¼ tsp thyme
¼ tsp oregano
1 tsp Lawry's seasoning salt
salt and pepper to taste
16 oz tomato sauce (2 small cans)

Brush eggplant with oil and bake in a hot oven (450 degrees) until light brown in color. Slit eggplant from end to end and let stand while you make stuffing. In a skillet, combine meat and garlic and cook till browned. Add remaining ingredients, except tomato sauce, and cook an additional 5-10 minutes. Remove from heat and fill eggplant with stuffing. Arrange in a baking pan and pour tomato sauce over each eggplant. Bake for about 30 minutes at 375 degrees. May be served hot or cold, sliced as an appetizer, whole as an entrée or as a meatless vegetable dish.

Turkey Tech Casserole

1 ½ lbs ground turkey
1 medium onion (chopped)
3 medium potatoes (cooked and diced)
3 T butter or margarine
½ c apple (diced)
½ c celery (chopped)
1 c zucchini (chopped)
1 c bread crumbs
2 egg yolks (beaten)

½ c milk
1 tsp salt
¼ tsp thyme
¼ tsp garlic powder
⅛ tsp sage
1 ½ c turkey gravy
¼ tsp pepper
⅛ tsp crushed red pepper
1 tsp parsley
1 T vermouth

In a skillet, sauté the first 3 ingredients in butter. Add apple, celery and zucchini. Sauté an additional 3-5 minutes. Mix in remaining ingredients carefully so as to not break up potatoes. Place in a well-buttered baking dish and bake at 350 degrees for 45 minutes. Garnish with fresh chopped parsley and paprika.

This dish may be served as an entrée with French bread and salad. It would also be excellent for brunch as an unusual side with poached eggs.

Classic Japanese Curry

Serves: 4-6

3 c raw chicken or pork (boned
    and chopped)
1/2 tsp chili powder
1 1/2 tsp curry powder
1/4 tsp turmeric
1/4 tsp cinnamon
1 tsp soy sauce

1/2 tsp dry mustard
1 medium onion (chopped)
1 T vegetable oil
2 potatoes (peeled and cubed)
1 1/2 c milk
juice of 1/2 lemon
4-6 c rice (cooked)

In a mixing bowl, combine meat, chili powder, curry, turmeric, cinnamon, soy sauce and dry mustard. In a skillet, sauté onion in a small amount of oil until tender. Add meat mixture and potatoes, cooking over low heat till meat begins to brown. Add 1/2 of the milk and cook 5-8 minutes or until slightly thickened. Add remaining milk and lemon juice and cook an additional 10 minutes.

Serve over hot cooked rice. I like curry because it is a spicey dish that gives you a warm feeling even on cold weather days. Condiments make it a build-your-own entrée to expand your pregame entertainment.

Condiments: Japanese and otherwise
Chopped nuts, sliced water chestnuts, grated egg, chopped green onion, shredded coconut, carrots, baby shrimp, raisins, peanuts, sliced bananas, chopped tomato, bean sprouts, sliced mushrooms, chutney, etc.

Crab Halibut Casserole

Serves: 6-8

¼ c onion or leeks (chopped)
3 T butter or margarine
1 (3 oz) can chopped mushrooms
(reserve liquid)
½ c cracker crumbs (about 12
saltines)
2 T parsley (chopped)

1 lb cooked crab or shrimp
4 T butter or margarine
4 T flour
milk and mushroom liquid to
equal 1½ c
⅓ c dry white wine
4-6 halibut fillets

In a skillet, sauté onion in butter until tender. Stir in mushrooms, crackers, parsley and crab. Simmer 3-5 minutes and set aside.

In a medium saucepan, combine butter and flour. Stir constantly over medium heat until butter has melted and begins to sizzle. Pour in milk and white wine. Continue stirring until mixture comes to a boil and thickens.

Place 2-3 fillets in the bottom of a casserole pan and spread with crab filling. Top with remaining fillets and cover with wine sauce. Bake in a 400 degree oven for 45 minutes. This is an extremely succulent casserole but not for the light eater.

Viking Casserole

Serves: 8

2 c rice
2 lbs ground beef
2 medium onions (chopped)
2 green or red bell peppers
(chopped)
2 T olive or vegetable oil
2 tsp salt
1 tsp pepper
¼ tsp garlic powder

¼ c soy sauce
4 c fresh or frozen whole kernel
corn
4 large tomatoes (sliced)
1 c fresh mushrooms (sliced)
1 c bread crumbs
3 T Parmesan cheese
1 T fresh parsley (chopped)

Prepare rice according to package directions. Set aside. Sauté beef, onion and peppers in oil. Cook until meat is browned. Season with salt, pepper, garlic and soy. In a large casserole dish, arrange layers of beef, corn, tomatoes and mushrooms. Finally, top with bread crumbs, Parmesan cheese and parsley. Bake for 30-35 minutes at 325 degrees. Wrap and serve hot at gametime beside rice, pasta, or on an open-faced toasted French roll or hamburger bun. This casserole is perfect for a blustery winter day.

Veggie Lasagna

Serves: 8-10

10 lasagna noodles
1 lb fresh spinach
2 c fresh mushrooms (sliced)
1 c carrots (grated)
³/4 c onion (chopped)
2 T olive oil
2 T vermouth
1 (15 oz) can tomato sauce

1 (6 oz) can tomato paste
¹/2 c black olives (chopped coarse)
1 tsp oregano (crushed)
1 tsp basil
2 c (16 oz) low fat cottage cheese
1 lb Monterey Jack cheese (grated)
¹/2 c Parmesan cheese (grated)

Cook noodles 8-10 minutes, then drain and rinse. Rinse spinach well and steam in a covered saucepan 3-5 minutes. Drain well and set aside.

In a large saucepan, sauté mushrooms, carrots and onion in olive oil until tender. Add vermouth. Stir in tomato sauce, paste, olives, oregano and basil. In a greased 13x9 inch baking pan, layer tomato sauce, noodles, cottage cheese, spinach and Parmesan cheese. Repeat layers, finishing with tomato sauce and cheeses. Bake in a 375 degree oven for 30 minutes then let stand for 10 minutes before serving. This is good served with garlic bread, an antipasta platter and salad.

Variation: If you have a summer garden add 1 c of sliced fresh zucchini to mushroom mixture. It's a great way to use them if you're facing a zucchini explosion. This lasagna freezes well.

Brunchbury Casserole

Serves: 8

6 slices whole wheat or sour dough bread
2 T butter or margarine
4 eggs (beaten)
1 c Mozzarella cheese (grated)
1 c Fontina cheese (grated)
1 small jar artichoke hearts (drained and chopped)
1 c fresh mushrooms (chopped)
2 T pimientos (chopped)
1 tsp dry mustard
1 tsp paprika
1 tsp salt
1 tsp Italian seasoning
1 c Ricotta cheese
2 cans evaporated milk

Trim crusts from the bread and place bread slices in a buttered 9x13 inch baking pan. Pour eggs into baking pan. Mix remaining ingredients and pour over eggs and bread. Bake in a 350 degree oven for 45 minutes. Let stand at least 10 minutes before serving and garnish with parsley and sliced tomatoes. This may be refrigerated up to 12 hours before cooking. Excellent as a brunch idea for early morning events. May be garnished with parsley and sliced tomatoes.

Variation: Top with homemade or prepared salsa.

Barbecued Lima Beans

Serves: 6-8

1 ham hock
7 c water
2 c large white lima beans
1 onion (chopped)
1 bell pepper (chopped) (optional)
3-4 cloves garlic (crushed)
1½ tsp chili powder
2 T olive or vegetable oil
1 can (8 oz) tomato sauce
1 small can tomato paste
2 T Worcestershire sauce
2 tsp prepared mustard
¼ c vinegar
dash of Tabasco to taste

In a large pot, precook ham hock for about 1 hour. Add remaining ingredients and simmer 1-2 hours until beans are tender.

Variation: Add ¼ c honey to beans for more a baked bean flavor.

World Cup Pasta

1 lb Linguini noodles (cooked and hot)
3 T olive oil
½ c asparagus tips (sliced diagonally)
6 green onions (chopped)
½ c celery (sliced diagonally)
½ c zucchini (sliced)
½ c mushrooms (sliced)
½ c fresh snow peas
1 c cream (heated but not to a boil)

1 c Fontina cheese (grated)
1 c Mozzarella cheese (grated)
1 c Romano cheese (grated)
3 sprigs fresh oregano (chopped) or 2 tsp dry
5-6 basil leaves (chopped) or 2 tsp dry
3 sprigs parsley (chopped) or 2 tsp dry
pepper to taste

In olive oil, sauté asparagus, onion, celery, zucchini, mushrooms and snow peas until barely tender. Keep warm while grating cheeses. Add vegetables, cream and cheeses to hot pasta. Toss with oregano, basil, parsley and pepper. Garnish if desired with fresh chopped tomatoes, pimientos or more fresh parsley. Cover and serve hot. I like to reheat this pasta in a large cast iron pan on low for late guests. This could also be done for a tailgate on a barbecue over low coals.

Border-Style Scalloped Potatoes

Serves: 8

½ lb Hot-style or Cajun sausage (cut into 1 inch pieces)
1 large onion (chopped)
2 T butter or margarine
2 c raw potatoes (thinly sliced)
2 c Monterey Jack or Cheddar cheese (grated)
½ (4 oz) can mild green chiles (chopped)
1 can condensed cream of mushroom soup

In a skillet, brown sausage and cook onions until tender. Butter a 2 quart baking dish or casserole and alternate layers of potatoes, sausage mixture, cheese, chiles and soup. Cover and bake at 325 degrees for 65 minutes or until potatoes are tender. Garnish with chopped chiles, olives and cilantro. You may wish to serve sour cream and mashed avocados on the side.

Easy Enchilada Casserole

Serves: 4-6

½ c onion (chopped)
2 tsp oil
dash of cayenne pepper
2 cloves garlic (crushed)
½ tsp chili powder
½ c water
1 can cream of mushroom soup
1 dozen tortillas, corn or flour

1 lb chicken, turkey, beef or ½ lb crab meat (cooked and shredded)
½ lb Cheddar cheese (grated)
1 small can green chiles (chopped)
2 T cilantro (chopped)

In a skillet, sauté onions in oil until tender. Stir in cayenne, garlic and chili powder. Add water to mushroom soup. In a buttered casserole dish layer tortillas, meat, onions, soup, cheese and chiles. Sprinkle with cilantro and bake at 350 degrees for 30 minutes.

Salmon Broccoli Quiche

Serves: 6

3 T onion (chopped)
¾ c broccoli (chopped)
2 T butter or margarine
4 eggs (beaten)
1 can evaporated milk
½ tsp basil

2 dashes curry
salt and pepper to taste
1 c Monterey Jack cheese (grated)
½ c salmon (drained and
   deboned)
1 (9 inch) deep dish pie crust

In a skillet, sauté onion and broccoli in butter until just tender. Set aside. Blend eggs, milk and herbs together. Add broccoli, salmon and cheese. Pour into pie crust. Bake on a cookie sheet for 45-55 minutes at 350 degrees. Center should be firm and set. Let stand for 10 minutes before serving. This is a good make-ahead item as it can be served hot or cold as an entrée or appetizer. It would be sumptuous for a brunch-type party and easy to transport for a tailgate.

Variation: Substitute shrimp, lobster or crab for salmon.

Arts, Zukes and Toms

Serves: 6-8

½ c olive oil
⅓ c vinegar
2 tsp Italian seasoning
3 cloves garlic (crushed)
1 tsp salt
½ tsp pepper
4 medium zukes (zucchini)
   (cut into ½ inch slices)

1 (8 oz) jar marinated artichoke
   hearts
2 large toms (tomatoes) (sliced)
1 T parsley (chopped fine)
Parmesan cheese (optional)

In a mixing bowl, wire whip oil, vinegar, seasoning, garlic, salt and pepper. Add zucchini and artichokes. Chill at least 4-6 hours or overnight. For service, mound zucchini mixture on a platter with a slotted spoon. Arrange tomatoes around. Drizzle extra marinade over tomatoes. Sprinkle with parsley and Parmesan cheese. Then dig in!

Baseball Wellington

Serves: 4

4 T blue cheese (crumbled)
4 T Worcestershire sauce
½ tsp basil
salt and pepper to taste
4 baseball steaks or filet mignons
1 Pepperidge Farms frozen puffed sheet (thawed)

Place blue cheese, Worcestershire sauce, basil, salt and pepper on top of each steak. Roll out puffed sheet and cut into quarters. Place one steak on each piece of pastry, cover and pinch edges around steak. Place on a broiling pan and bake at 450 degrees for 12-14 minutes on highest oven rack for rare steak, or 20 minutes for well done. Serve with Bordelaise or Bearnaise Sauce mentioned in this book.

Seafood Florentine

Serves: 8

2 (10 oz) pkgs frozen spinach
(chopped, thawed and drained)
½ c butter or margarine
⅓ c flour
1 tsp salt
½ c milk
1 can evaporated milk
4 tsp lemon juice
2 egg yolks (beaten)
6 oz crab meat
4 oz cooked shrimp
4 oz cooked fish (like cod)
½ c walnuts or pecans (chopped coarse)
2 c bread crumbs (soft)
½ c Parmesan cheese

Spread spinach in the bottom of a well greased baking dish or cast iron pan. Melt ½ c butter in a saucepan over low heat and blend in flour and salt, using a wire whisk. Gradually add milk and cook until thickened. Remove from heat and add lemon juice. Combine a small amount of sauce with egg yolks and add this to remaining sauce mixture. Blend in crab, shrimp, fish and walnuts, then pour over spinach mixture in baking pan. Sprinkle bread crumbs and Parmesan cheese evenly over top of crab mixture. Bake for 15-20 minutes at 350 degrees or until golden brown.

Cheesey Potatoes

Serves: 6

6 medium potatoes
5 T butter or margarine (softened)
1 c Caraway cheese (grated)
²/₃ c sour cream
¼ c green onion (chopped)

2 dashes Worcestershire sauce
salt and pepper to taste
2-3 slices bacon (cooked and
crumbled)

Wash potatoes, dry and wrap each individually in tin foil.

In a covered container, mix remaining ingredients and keep refrigerated until service. Heat potatoes in oven, barbecue on top of grill or in coals until soft when pierced with a fork. Remove from oven or coals and make crisscross scores through the tin foil. Turn back the points of the foil and slit open potatoes. Top with sour cream mixture.

Other options to mix in: avocado, blue cheese, salsa, smoked oysters or marinated artichoke hearts.

Time Saver: Microwave the potatoes about 10 minutes before wrapping in foil, then heat on barbecue until soft.

Refried Beans

Serves: 8-10

2¹/₂ c dry pinto beans
6 c water
2 slices bacon

1¹/₂ tsp salt
1 clove garlic (crushed)
2 T vegetable oil

In a pot, bring beans to a boil for 4 minutes and let stand for 1 hour. Drain and cover beans with fresh water. Add remaining ingredients, except oil, and cook slowly for another hour or until beans are soft. In a skillet, heat oil and add several large spoonfuls of fairly drained beans. Mash about ¹/₂ of beans with a potato masher as they fry. Stir frequently until heated throughout and serve topped with grated Monterey Jack cheese.

These beans can be frozen for dips and Mexican dishes 2-3 weeks ahead of time.

Green Chile Rice

Serves: 8

3 medium zucchini (thinly sliced)
1 c rice (cooked)
1 (7½ oz) can green chiles
  (chopped)
12 oz Monterey Jack cheese
  (grated)
1 large tomato (thinly sliced)

2 c sour cream
1 tsp oregano
1 tsp garlic powder
¼ c bell pepper (chopped)
¼ c green onion (chopped)
2 T fresh basil or 1 tsp dried basil
salt and pepper to taste

Blanch zucchini until just tender. In a buttered casserole, layer in order rice, chiles, ½ the cheese, zucchini and tomatoes. Combine sour cream, oregano, garlic powder, bell pepper, onion and basil. Spoon evenly over tomato layer. Sprinkle with remaining cheese and bake at 350 degrees for 50 minutes. May be garnished with chopped parsley. This is a terrific side dish with grilled meat or chicken.

Guy-U-Pintas

Serves: 6-8

1 c dried pink beans
2 onions (chopped)
1 coconut with milk
2 c long grain rice

1 tsp of thyme
dash of cayenne
salt and pepper to taste

In a pot, bring beans to a boil for 4 minutes and remove from heat for 1 hour. Drain and cover with fresh water. Add onions then simmer approximately 1 hour until beans are soft. With a hammer, punch a hole in coconut and empty milk into a bowl. Break up coconut and dig out coconut meat. Cut coconut meat into small pieces and put into blender or food processor to shred. Add milk and shredded coconut to beans along with remaining ingredients. Cover and simmer an additional 20 minutes or until rice is done. Add a little water if necessary for fluffy rice.

This item is good as a novel side dish with beef or turtle meat.

Serve with Tabasco and a wedge of lime. What can I say? "It's a Costa Rican Recipe," and who knows, you may stumble across a turtle just before the game. (Just in case you don't have a steak or two ready.)

Substitute: In place of one coconut with milk, add 1 small can unsweetened coconut milk and ½ small pkg unsweetened shredded coconut.

Turkey Enchiladas   Serves: 6-8

1 (8 oz) can tomato sauce
1 (7 oz) can taco sauce
1 (10 oz) can enchilada sauce
1 (8 oz) can El Pato tomato sauce
1 lb turkey or chicken (cooked
    and shredded)

1 small can olives (chopped)
¾ lb cheese (grated) Monterey
    Jack, Cheddar or Mozzarella
1 c onions (chopped)
1 dozen flour or 1½ dozen corn
tortillas

In a saucepan, simmer first 4 ingredients for about 15 minutes. Cool. Mix remaining ingredients except tortillas, keeping out ¼ of the cheese. When sauce is cool enough to touch, take 1 tortilla at a time and douse both sides in sauce. Fill with 2 T of turkey mixture and roll tortilla, starting at one end. Place in a greased baking dish (11x13 inch) and ladle remaining sauce over enchiladas. Sprinkle with remaining cheese and bake in a 400 degree oven for 20 minutes. Serve hot. May be garnished with chervil, sliced olives, green onions, crumbled bacon or sour cream.

Very Original Tamale Pie

Everyone has an old family recipe. This one is written pretty much as it was given to me.

1 c corn meal	¼ tsp garlic powder
2¼ c milk	¼ tsp pepper
1 (6 oz) can medium pitted olives (drained)	1 large onion (chopped)
	1½ lbs cooked ground beef
1 (25 oz) can whole or stewed tomatoes	2 eggs
	1 (8 oz) can whole kernel corn (drained)
1 T chili powder	
½ tsp salt	1½ c Cheddar cheese (grated)

In a small bowl, stir corn meal into milk and allow to soak while mixing "rest of goop." Combine remaining ingredients in a large bowl, omitting cheese. Add milk mixture and stir well. Pour into a 9x13 inch lightly-greased baking dish and cook for ½ hour at 375 degrees. Remove from oven and sprinkle liberally with Cheddar cheese. Bake another 30-45 minutes and let rest for 10 minutes before service. This is an ideal tailgate food because it retains heat during transport and is a hearty enough cold weather food "to bring 'em back for more."

Los Lobos Casserole

Serves: 6

1 c half & half
2 eggs
⅓ c flour
3 c canned chiles (whole)

½ lb Monterey Jack cheese
½ lb Sharp Cheddar cheese
8 oz homemade or prepared salsa

In a mixing bowl, beat together half & half, eggs and flour. Pour into a greased casserole. Layer with chiles, cheese and salsa. Bake at 325 degrees for 45 minutes. Travels well for a tailgate.

Zucchini Tomato Sauté

Serves: 6-8

2 T olive or vegetable oil
½ medium onion (quartered)
4 medium zucchinis (cut julienne-style)
2 medium tomatoes (coarse chopped)

½ tsp rosemary
¼ tsp salt
fresh ground pepper to taste
2 T dry white wine

Heat skillet over medium to medium high heat and add oil. Wait a minute then add onions and brown lightly. Add remaining ingredients and sauté an additional 3-5 minutes. This is wonderful served beside or over barbecue fish steaks.

Variations:
1. Add 1 clove crushed garlic to sautéed vegetables
2. Add 1 T fresh or ½ tsp dry basil or oregano
3. When barbecuing, this dish may be prepared in a cast iron skillet on the barbecue grill.

Freestyle Brandied Yams

6 medium yams
4 T butter or margarine
1 apple (cored and thinly sliced)
½ c brown sugar

1 tsp cinnamon
¼ tsp cloves
½ tsp nutmeg
⅓ c brandy

Wash, peel and slice yams. Steam about 7 minutes and drain. In a buttered baking dish, arrange yam and apple slices, then dot with butter. Mix remaining ingredients in saucepan and simmer about 15 minutes. Pour over yams and bake 35 minutes at 325 degrees.

Option: Sprinkle with chopped walnuts or almonds.

Chili for a Crowd

We're talking about an ARMY!

5 qts dry kidney beans
6 lbs ground beef
4 c onions (chopped)
3 c bell pepper (chopped)
15 cloves garlic (crushed)
½ c oil
8 c whole or stewed canned
    tomatoes

2 qts tomato sauce
½ c chili powder
3 T cumin or cuminos
1 T crushed red pepper
1 tsp Tabasco
salt and pepper to taste

In the largest pot you can find (you're cooking for masses) cover beans with boiling water and boil an additional 3 minutes. Set aside. In a big skillet, sauté beef, onions and garlic in oil until browned. Add beef mixture and remaining ingredients to beans. Cook slowly for about 2-3 hours or until beans are soft. Stir occasionally. May be topped with Parmesan cheese before serving. Serve with tortillas, sour dough bread or crackers on the side.

4 Bean Casserole

Serves: 20 plus

2 medium onions (chopped)
3 T olive or vegetable oil
1 lb ham (chopped)
1 (16 oz) can lima beans (drained)
1 (16 oz) can garbanzo beans (drained)
1 (16 oz) can pork & beans

1 (15½ oz) can kidney beans (drained)
2 fresh tomatoes (chopped)
¼ c honey
2 T Worcestershire sauce
½ tsp dry or prepared mustard
½ tsp basil

Sauté onions in oil until tender. Place ham, onion and remaining ingredients into a casserole dish. Bake covered at 375 degrees for 40 minutes. Uncover and bake an additional 20 minutes to desired consistency. Wrap securely and serve hot at gametime.

Scalloped Potatoes

Serves: 8

8-10 medium red potatoes (sliced)
1 medium onion (sliced)
⅓ c butter
¼ tsp cayenne pepper
1 c evaporated milk

1 can mushroom soup
salt and pepper to taste
⅓ c Parmesan cheese
2 T fresh parsley (chopped)

Preheat oven to 350 degrees. In a buttered baking dish, layer potatoes and onions, dotting with butter. In a separate bowl, mix cayenne, milk, soup, salt and pepper. Pour over potatoes and top with Parmesan cheese and parsley. Bake 45 minutes until potatoes are tender. This is great at home or taken to a winter tailgate.

Eggplant Parmesan

1 cup onions (chopped)
3 T olive or vegetable oil
1 cup red or green bell pepper
   (chopped)
1 clove garlic (crushed)
2 tsp basil
1 tsp oregano
1 T parsley
1 bay leaf (crumbled)
1 (13 oz) can tomato puree

1 (6 oz) can tomato paste
⅓ c white wine and brandy
   (½ wine and ½ brandy)
1 cup fresh tomatoes (chopped)
2 medium eggplant (peeled and
   sliced)
½ lb Cheddar cheese (grated)
½ lb Mozzarella cheese (grated)
½ cup Parmesan cheese
salt to taste

In a large pot, sauté onions in oil until tender. Stir in the next 10 ingredients and simmer for ½ hour. Assemble casserole in a 9x13 inch baking dish, alternate layers of tomato mixture, eggplant and cheeses. Top with a final layer of tomato and cheeses and bake at 375 degrees for 30 minutes. May be served hot as an entrée or cold as an appetizer.

Variations:
1. Add ½ c mushrooms (sliced) to tomato mixture.
2. Add 1 lb cooked ground beef to tomato mixture.

SANDWICHES

Stands Fans
Submarine Sandwich

Serves: 4-6

The submarine sandwich has been a part of American sporting events for some time now. It was probably one of the original tailgate menu items, so can't be ignored in this book. Today's submarine concoctions have gone beyond simple meat and cheese hoagies and have become gourmet marvels in their own right. Here are just a few ideas for combinations, spreads and sandwiches. A time-saver when you have a big group is to have everyone bring their favorite sandwich meat, cheese, etc. and design your menu around a sandwich bar theme. It's easy for you and stimulates the old gastronomical imagination.

Submarine Sandwich Bar

Assorted Breads and Rolls: White, wheat, rye, Kaiser rolls, pocket bread, Pumpernickle, French, hoagie buns, English muffins, biscuits, croissants, dinner rolls, tortillas or waffles.

Fillings and Stuff: Lox, cream cheese, roast beef, thin-sliced steak, roast pork, turkey, bologna, ham, pastrami, corned beef, chicken, tuna, ham, egg and salmon salads, lettuces, spinach, tomato, wax peppers, white and red onion, assorted thin-sliced cheeses, marinated artichokes, cucumber, liverwurst, chorizo, summer and other sausages, green and black olives, crab, shrimp or calamari. Let your imagination go wild.

Vegetarian Sandwich Bar

Assorted Breads and Rolls: White, wheat, Kaiser rolls, French bread or rolls, pocket bread, corn bread, biscuits, croissants, date bread, banana, zucchini or other breads or rolls.

Fillings and Stuff: Assorted cheeses, alfalfa and mixed sprouts, tomatoes, bell pepper, sliced egg, tuna or salmon salad, cooked shrimp, cream cheese and spreads thereof, sliced green or black olives, peanut butter, red and white onion, cucumbers, pickles, wax peppers, bean or garbanzo spreads, lettuces, fresh mushrooms, caviar, capers and/or avocado. For those who eat poultry: chicken, turkey, duck, smoked pheasant, poultry patés.

Build Your Own Peanut Butter Masterpiece

This menu could be the basis of a great little-kid theme party.

Mixed Breads: Whole wheat, white, French, bagels, English muffins, graham crackers, or even quick breads like banana and zucchini.

Peanut butter and other suggestions: Various jellies, preserves and jams, banana, butter, pickles, potato chips, fresh pineapple, bacon, marshmallow cream, fresh apple slices, chocolate chips, chopped or whole peanuts or other nuts, mini marshmallows, gum drops, mayonnaise, honey, celery or other fresh fruits or vegetables.

Italian Turkey Sandwich
Serves: 4-6

1 loaf French bread (sliced
   horizontally)
¼ c mayonnaise
8 oz Ricotta cheese
1 tsp celery salt
3-4 cloves garlic (crushed)
½ tsp pepper

3 hard boiled eggs (chopped)
½ bunch fresh spinach (cleaned
   and patted dry)
½ lb turkey (thinly sliced)
1 can black olives (sliced and
   drained)
½ red onion (thinly sliced)

Spread bread with mayonnaise and set aside. In a small mixing bowl, combine Ricotta cheese, celery salt, garlic, pepper and egg. Spread onto one side of bread and follow with layers of spinach, turkey, olives and onion. Wrap and refrigerate until service.

Variations:
1. May use thin-sliced salami in addition to turkey.
2. Add dill pickles, sliced tomatoes and wax peppers.

Meatball Sandwiches

Makes: approx 30 meatballs
or 10 sandwiches

Sauce

16 oz tomato sauce
½ cucumber (chopped)
4 fresh tomatoes (chopped)
1 large onion (chopped)
1 small bell pepper (chopped)
¼ c parsley (chopped)
1 tsp Worcestershire sauce
1 tsp thyme
½ tsp oregano
1 clove garlic (crushed)

Meatballs

2 lbs ground beef
1 c cracker or bread crumbs
1 T Italian seasoning
1 tsp soy sauce
2 tsp Lawry's seasoning salt
½ c onion (chopped)
¼ c parsley (chopped)
1 medium tomato (chopped)
½ bell pepper (chopped)
10 slices Mozzarella cheese
10 French or hoagie rolls

In a covered container, combine ingredients for sauce and refrigerate until service. Prepare meatballs by mixing meat, bread crumbs, spices, tomato and bell pepper together and forming 3 inch meatballs. Place meatballs in a baking pan and bake 25-30 minutes at 350 degrees. Serve hot in French rolls with cheese and sauce.

All in One Sandwich

3 to 3½ c flour
1 tsp salt
1 pkg dry yeast
1½ c hot water (125-130 degrees)

4 tsp oil
2 T sesame or caraway seeds
egg wash (1 egg and 2 T water, beaten)

In a large mixing bowl, combine 2½ c flour, salt and yeast. Stir in hot water and oil. Mix in remaining flour and caraway or sesame seeds to make a soft dough. Knead bread for about 5-8 minutes on a floured surface. Roll bread dough out into a rectangle about 1 inch thick and cut 1 inch diagonal strips ⅓ of the way along both long sides. Fill with layers of filling described below. Weave outer strips of bread over filling to form a criss-cross effect. Cover dough and let rest for about 20-25 minutes. Brush loaf with an egg wash and bake in a 400 degree oven for about 25-30 minutes. This loaf can be wrapped and taken to the game hot or sliced and served cold with hot soup and a salad. You can also divide the dough into 4-6 pieces and make hand held loaves for each of your guests.

Fillings
1. ½ lb sliced ham
   ¼ lb sliced Cheddar cheese
   ½ c mustard with ¼ tsp curry mixed in

2. ½ lb sliced roast beef
   1 medium onion (thinly sliced)
   ¼ c bell pepper slices
   ½ c marinated mushrooms (drained and thinly sliced)
   ¼ lb sliced Monterey Jack cheese
   ½ c flavored mustard or try French dressing

3. ½ c Dijon-style mustard
   ½ lb pastrami (thinly sliced)
   ¼ lb Swiss cheese (thinly sliced)
   4-5 dill pickles (thinly sliced)
   8 oz can sauerkraut (drained)
   1-2 green onions (chopped)

Nutty Cream Cheese Sandwich Spread

Serves: 6-8

3 (8 oz) pkgs cream cheese (softened)
½ c walnuts (chopped)
¼ c unsalted sunflower seeds
1 small can olives (chopped)

3 green onions (chopped)
1 small clove garlic (crushed)
¼ c lemon juice
¼ tsp Cajun seasoning

In a mixing bowl or food processor with plastic blade, combine all ingredients until well mixed. Refrigerate until gametime or spread onto sandwich rolls and top with tomato, sprouts, lettuce and sliced red onion. This is a recipe limited only by your imagination.

Variations:
1. Substitute 1 c grated cheddar cheese for 1 pkg cream cheese and add a 2 oz jar of diced pimientos.
2. Add ½ c shrimp to the mixture to make a shrimp spread.

Cracker Bread Rolls

Makes: 12-14

2 pieces cracker bread (14 inch diameter)
water
2 avocados (mashed with 2 T lemon juice)
¼ c mint or cilantro (chopped)
salt, pepper and Tabasco sauce to taste
⅔ c chopped almonds

1 lb turkey (thinly sliced)
1⅓ c cucumber (thinly sliced)
⅓ c black olives (sliced or chopped)
1 red onion (thinly sliced)
1 pkg fresh alfalfa sprouts
2 c Monterey Jack cheese (thinly sliced)

Hold cracker bread one at a time under gently running water, wetting both sides. Seal flat in a plastic wrap. Let stand until soft enough to roll (about 45 minutes). Mix together avocados, mint, salt, pepper and Tabasco. Spread each cracker with ½ of avocado mixture and layer with remaining ingredients as filling. Roll crackers into a jellyroll shape and slice into pinwheel sandwiches.

Variations:
1. Refried beans, ground beef, tomato, lettuce, olives and mashed avocado.
2. Cream cheese, olives, green onion, alfalfa sprouts and walnuts.
3. Fresh spinach, grated egg, marinated mushrooms, shrimp, Dijon-style mustard and mayonnaise mixture.

The possibilities are endless. You just need to be creative and use ingredients that will sort of stick together when you cut the rolls.

Barbecued Oriental
Chicken Sandwich
Makes: 4

4 chicken breasts (boned)	1 clove garlic (crushed)
¼ c soy sauce	2 small onions (quartered)
1 tsp sugar	1 bell pepper (cut into eighths)
1 tsp ground ginger	wooden skewers
½ tsp grated lemon peel	4 Kaiser rolls
2 T lemon juice	fresh chopped napa cabbage
¼ tsp dry mustard	

In a covered container place chicken breasts, soy sauce, sugar, ginger, lemon peel and lemon juice to marinate. Marinate meat for 4-6 hours or over night.

Cut chicken breasts into 5-6 pieces each and skewer with onion and bell pepper. Retain marinade and use to baste chicken while cooking. Refrigerate until gametime. Barbecue skewered chicken 10-15 minutes, turning and basting frequently. Toast rolls, remove chicken from skewers, and place meat, vegetables and cabbage in rolls. Use any remaining marinade as a dip for sandwiches.

Crab Carries

½ lb fresh cooked or canned
    crab (drained)
½ c green onion (chopped)
½ c celery (chopped)
6 strips bacon (crisped and
    crumbled)

1 c Cheddar cheese (grated)
1 tsp parsley or cilantro (chopped)
½ c mayonnaise
2 T catsup
½ tsp horseradish
6-8 English muffin halves

Combine all ingredients and place on top of English muffins. Broil 10-15 minutes or wrap individually in foil, carry to game and heat on barbecue grill approximately 10 minutes. May be served cold or hot.

Stuffed French Bread Sandwiches

French bread is a wonderful sports-party item because of its versatility. It can be stuffed with almost anything, heated, wrapped and served warm in the winter or filled with cool fresh vegetables and meats during the summer. Here are ideas to get you started.

4-6 medium French bread rolls

Fillings
1. ½ lb Swiss, Provolone or Caraway cheese (sliced)
   ¼ lb ham (sliced)
   ¼ lb mushrooms (chopped)
   3 T Dijon or other flavored mustard
   1-2 green onions (chopped)
   3 T mayonnaise

2. ½ lb jalapeño pepper cheese (diced)
   ¼ lb cooked chorizo sausage (casing removed)
   ¼ lb cooked chicken (diced)
   1-2 green onions (chopped)
   1 bell pepper (thinly sliced)
   1 tomato (thinly sliced)
   3-4 T mayonnaise or sour cream

3. 1-2 cans drained tuna or 1 lb cooked shrimp
   ½ lb Monterey Jack or Mozzarella cheese
   1 large dill pickle (chopped)
   1 stalk celery (chopped)
   ¼ c mayonnaise

Cut the top off the rolls and hollow out the center. Fill rolls with ingredients for fillings and put top back onto rolls. Serve cold or wrap in foil and heat for about 30 minutes at 325 degrees. In the winter these can be a warm and hearty accompaniment to homemade soup.

Italian Sandwich Spread

Makes: 2½ c

1 (5 oz) jar dried beef (chopped)
8 oz cream cheese (softened)
1 tsp basil
2 cloves garlic (crushed)

¼ c Dijon-style mustard
¼ c chives or green onion
   (chopped)

Blend ingredients in a food processor or by hand, until smooth.
Thinly spread on your choice of bread or rolls and top with sliced tomatoes and leaf lettuce.

Pita Pocket Sandwiches

2 T butter or margarine
1 lb chicken breast (cooked and
    thinly sliced)
½ onion (chopped)
1 clove garlic (crushed)
1 T chili powder
1 small zucchini (cut julienne)
1 small can sliced or chopped
    black olives

Package and take to game:
6 pita bread halves (wrap in foil
    to heat if desired)
2 c Monterey Jack or Cheddar
    cheese (grated)
2 tomatoes (sliced)
2 avocados (sliced and dipped in
    lemon juice)
6 leaves red lettuce (cleaned and
    patted dry)
Italian dressing (optional)

In a skillet, sauté sliced chicken lightly in butter. Stir in onion, garlic and chili powder, cooking until onions are tender. Add zucchini and olives. Continue to heat 2-3 more minutes. Place mixture in a covered container and serve hot at gametime.

To assemble sandwiches: Heat pita bread in tin foil over barbecue for 1-2 minutes or until warm. Pitas may be used either hot or cold. Cut in half and fill with hot meat mixture, cheese, tomato, avocado and lettuce. Drizzle with a little Italian dressing and chow down.

Variation: Substitute ground beef or thinly sliced steak for chicken and barbecue at gametime. Marinate meat for a further flavor twist.

Tarragon Dill Lobster Sandwich

1 c lobster or shrimp (cooked, deveined, chopped)
½ tsp lemon juice
¼ c mayonnaise
2 T green onions (chopped fine)
¼ tsp tarragon

salt and pepper to taste
¼ lb Havarti with dill or Monterey Jack cheese (thinly sliced)
2-4 English muffins, croissants or ½ loaf French bread

In a mixing bowl, combine first six ingredients and blend well. Fill muffins, top with cheese and heat thoroughly. These are served open-faced.

To barbecue: Place tops on sandwiches and wrap in foil. Refrigerate. Lay foil-wrapped sandwiches on barbecue for approximately 10 minutes, turning occasionally. This should wow YOUR fans. It's tasty and elegant.

Variation: Use puff pastry shells in place of bread and serve topped with cheese for a home-based party or if you have a motor home. Follow package directions for preparation of pastry shells.

Calzone

1½-2 c flour
1 pkg dry yeast
½ tsp salt
2/3 c warm water (115-120 degrees)
4 tsp oil

Filling
¼ lb ground beef
2 Italian sausages (remove casing and crumble)
1 medium onion (chopped)
1 clove garlic (crushed)
1 tsp basil
1 tsp Lawry's seasoning salt
4 slices Mozzarella or Provolone cheese
1 egg

Sauce
1 tsp oregano
1 tsp thyme
1 tsp marjoram
1 (8 oz) can tomato sauce
salt and pepper to taste

In a mixing bowl combine ²/₃ c flour, yeast and salt. Add warm water and oil and beat for 3-4 minutes. Mix in as much remaining flour as you can. On a lightly floured surface knead in enough remaining flour to make a smooth elastic dough (about 6-8 minutes). Cover and let rise till doubled (about 1 hour).

Prepare filling by cooking hamburger and sausage till browned. Add onion and garlic, cooking until tender. Drain excess fat and add tomato sauce. Cook an additional 10 minutes then set aside to cool.

Divide doubled dough into 4 pieces and let rest 5-10 minutes. On a floured surface, roll each piece into an 8 inch circle. Place circle onto greased baking sheet and fill one side with ¹/₂ cup meat filling. Top with 1 slice of cheese then moisten the edge with an egg wash (1 egg + 1 tsp water) and fold dough into a turnover shape, crimping edges closed with a fork. Prick dough once with fork and bake for 25 minutes at 375 degrees. Combine ingredients for sauce. Pour over or serve beside calzone as a dip. These also microwave very nicely.

NO TIME!! Use frozen bread dough as your base. Follow package directions for thawing, then use as you would homemade dough.

Barbecued Bratwurst Sandwich   Serves: 6-8

3-4 Bratwurst sausages
½ green bell pepper (chopped)
½ red bell pepper (chopped)
1-2 green onions (chopped)
1 tomato (chopped)
¼ lb mushrooms (sliced)

½ tsp dry mustard
1 tsp fennel seed
1 tsp cayenne pepper
2 T olive or vegetable oil
6-8 French rolls

Preboil bratwurst at home until firm to touch, about 8-10 minutes.

In a skillet, combine peppers, onion, tomato, mushrooms, mustard, fennel, cayenne and oil. Sauté until onion and peppers are tender. Barbecue or broil sausage until thoroughly heated. Slice into pieces and serve on toasted buns topped with vegetable mixture.

Barbecued Fajitas   Serves: 6

2 lbs flank or other steak
   (tenderized)
1 c dry red wine
juice of 1 lemon or lime
1 tsp garlic powder
¼ c soy sauce
1 onion (¼ inch sliced rounds)
1 bell pepper (¼ inch sliced
   rounds)

1 dozen flour tortillas (wrap in foil)
guacamole
fresh or prepared salsa
cilantro
sour cream

In a covered container, marinate flank steak in wine, lemon juice, garlic powder and soy sauce. Refrigerate 4 hours or overnight, turning occasionally. Wrap onions and peppers in foil and keep refrigerated until gametime.

Barbecue meat to desired doneness and heat wrapped tortillas, onions and bell peppers till warm on top of barbecue.

To assemble fajitas, slice flank steak into thin strips and place in center of warm tortilla along with guacamole, barbecue onion and bell pepper slices, salsa, sour cream and fresh cilantro. Roll tortilla around filling and enjoy.

Salmon Sandwich for 8

Serves: 8

1 loaf French bread (cut
  lengthwise)
12 oz cream cheese
4 medium tomatoes (thinly sliced)
1 cucumber (sliced)
½ lb smoked salmon (shredded
  and boned)

4 hardboiled eggs (sliced)
1 small red onion (thinly sliced)
8 small leaves romaine lettuce
¼ c mayonnaise

Layer bread with items listed above, beginning with cream cheese and ending with a bit of mayonnaise. This sandwich can be premade, wrapped and sliced for a tailgate or hotel party. With either, the order of the day is "Pig Out."

Spicey Sausage Sandwich

Serves: 6-8

1 T olive oil
1 lb spicey sausage (cut in 1 inch pieces)
½ bell pepper (sliced)
½ c fresh zucchini (sliced)
1 onion (sliced)
1 c fresh tomato (chopped)
½ tsp salt
½ tsp basil
½ tsp oregano
½ tsp pepper
1 loaf French bread (sliced horizontally)
½ c Monterey Jack cheese (shredded)
1 small can black olives (sliced)

In a skillet, heat oil and add next 9 ingredients. Reduce heat to low and simmer for about 20-30 minutes. Fill loaf with meat mixture and sprinkle with cheese and olives. Bake in a 400 degree oven for 15 minutes or until thoroughly heated. Or wrap tightly in foil and heat on barbecue over medium coals for about 20 minutes. Turn frequently.

Tuna/Egg Sandwich Filling

Makes: 2 c

1 can (7 oz) tuna (drained)
1 hard boiled egg (chopped)
½ c celery (chopped)
1 T pickle relish or chutney (chopped fine)
¼ c mayonnaise
¼ tsp dill weed
¼ tsp ground black pepper
¼ tsp or less curry powder (to taste)

Blend all ingredients together and chill until service. Serve on your choice of bread with red onion, lettuce and tomato.

Oriental Chicken Rolls

Crust

3-3½ c flour
1 pkg dry yeast
1 tsp salt
¾ c milk (warm)

2 eggs
¼ c oil
egg wash (beat together 1 egg and
   1 T water)

In a large mixing bowl, combine 2 c flour, yeast and salt. Stir in milk, eggs and oil. Beat with an electric mixer for 3 minutes, scraping bowl occasionally. With a spoon, stir in as much remaining flour as possible. On a lightly floured surface, knead to make a smooth elastic dough (6 minutes). Shape into a ball and place in greased bowl for about 1 hour or until doubled.

Prepare filling. Divide dough into 10-12 pieces. On a floured surface, roll into 4-6 inch circles and fill with 2-3 T of filling. Bring dough up around filling and pinch top to seal. Place rolls sealed side up on a greased baking sheet and brush with the egg wash. Let rise, covered, for another 30 minutes until doubled and bake for 15-20 minutes at 375 degrees.

NO TIME!!! Use frozen bread dough and follow package directions.

Oriental Chicken Filling

1 egg (beaten)
1 tsp vinegar
2 tsp soy sauce
1 T corn starch
2 tsp ginger (grated)
1 clove garlic (crushed)
¼ c bean sprouts (chopped)
¼ c celery (finely chopped)

1 carrot (finely chopped)
½ onion (finely chopped)
1 (6 oz) can mushrooms (drained
   and chopped)
1 c chicken or pork (cooked and
   chopped)
¼ c Chinese cabbage (chopped)

In a mixing bowl combine egg, vinegar, soy sauce, corn starch, ginger and garlic. Add remaining ingredients and mix well. Use to fill bundles.

Spinach Shrimp Filling

1 pkg (10 oz) frozen chopped
   spinach or broccoli (thawed
   and drained)
2 eggs (beaten)
½ c Mozzarella cheese (grated)
½ c cottage cheese
¼ c Provolone cheese

½ onion (chopped)
¼ c bread or cracker crumbs
1 tsp basil
1 clove garlic (crushed)
salt and pepper to taste
½ c shrimp (cooked)

Mix all ingredients and use to fill bundles.

Cheese and Beef Sandwich   Serves: 6-8

6-8 French rolls
2 lbs roast beef (thinly sliced)
1 lb jalapeño pepper cheese
   (thinly sliced)

1-2 tomatoes (thinly sliced)
2 avocados (peeled and sliced)
mayonnaise (optional)

Arrange roast beef on rolls and top with slices of cheese. Wrap in foil and heat about 10-12 minutes until cheese is melted. Serve hot with tomatoes, avocado and mayonnaise.

SAUCES

Teriyaki Sauce for a Mob

Makes: 1 qt

1 qt soy sauce
1 lb brown sugar
2 medium sliced oranges
2-3 fresh ginger roots (2-3 oz)
    grated

8 medium garlic cloves
1 T whole oregano
2 T dry mustard

In a saucepan, mix all ingredients and bring to a boil. Lower heat and simmer 5 minutes, stirring constantly. Strain and cool liquid. Store in a covered bottle or container in a cool place until use. For marinade: Marinate meat for 3 hours before barbecue. This is great to make at the beginning of the season for use or distribute among YOUR fans.

Sweet and Sour Sauce

Makes: 1½ c

½ c packed brown sugar
1 T cornstarch
¼ c plum wine
¼ c vinegar
⅓ c chicken broth

2 T soy sauce
1 clove garlic (crushed)
¼ tsp ginger
¼ c bell pepper (chopped fine)
2 T green onion (chopped fine)

In a small bowl, combine cornstarch and chicken broth. Wire whip until well blended. In a saucepan, combine all ingredients, including cornstarch mixture, and simmer over medium heat until thick and bubbly. May be used hot or cold on or beside chicken, ribs or meatballs. Garnish with more chopped green onion, red bell pepper or sliced fresh ginger.

Derby Bordelaise Sauce

Makes: 3 1/4 c

2/3 c fresh mushrooms (chopped)
2 T butter or margarine
3 T cornstarch
2 c beef stock

4 T red wine or Madiera
3 T fresh squeezed lemon juice
2 tsp tarragon
2 dashes pepper

In a skillet over medium heat, sauté mushrooms in butter until tender (about 2-3 minutes). Dissolve cornstarch in beef stock and add to mushrooms. Cook, stirring constantly, until mixture begins to boil. Add remaining ingredients. Reduce heat and simmer 5-10 additional minutes. Yummy over beef, lamb, etc.

Bearnaise Sauce

Makes: 1 1/4 c

1/4 c wine vinegar
1/4 c dry white wine
1 T shallots or green onions
   (minced)
1/2 T tarragon

1/2 tsp salt
1/8 tsp pepper
2/3 c butter or margarine
3 egg yolks
2 T cold butter or margarine

In a saucepan combine vinegar, wine, shallots, tarragon, salt and pepper. Cook over low heat until liquid is reduced to 2 T. Set aside to cool. Melt butter in another saucepan over low heat and also set aside.

Place egg yolks in double boiler and beat with fork until lemon colored. Set over hot non-boiling water and add 1 T of cold butter. Beat until slightly thickened. Remove from hot water and whip in second 1 T cold butter. Gradually add melted butter to yolk mixture, beating constantly. Return to double boiler, stirring until sauce is thickened. Add wine mixture to yolks and blend until well-mixed and heated. Serve over thin sliced meat, vegetables or brunch items.

Blender Lemon
Horseradish Sauce

Makes: 1 c

¼ c olive oil
2 T green onion (chopped)
2 eggs
½ tsp salt
¾ c sour cream

½ fresh lemon (grated peel and
  juice)
2-3 tsp prepared horseradish
¼ tsp ground black pepper

Blend all ingredients in blender until thoroughly combined. May be served cold or, if desired, heated prior to service over medium heat (do not boil). Either way it's great over hot/cold cooked asparagus, carrots, snow peas, etc. You can also use this as an interesting variation salad dressing.

Peanut Sauce

Makes: ½ c

¼ c peanut butter
2 tsp soy sauce
2 tsp water
¼ tsp sugar

2 dashes turmeric
1 clove garlic (crushed)
2 drops Tabasco

In a mixing bowl, combine all ingredients. Slowly add an additional ¼ cup water and blend until smooth. This sauce may be served hot or cold on thinly sliced beef or oriental chicken.

Mustard Sauce

2 T onions (minced)
1/2 c butter or margarine
1/2 c flour
1 1/2 c milk
1 c chicken stock

1/4 c vermouth
3 T lemon juice
2 T prepared German mustard
1 tsp sugar
1 tsp salt

In a saucepan, sauté onions with butter until tender. Stir in flour then gradually add milk, chicken stock and vermouth. Cook over medium heat, stirring constantly until thickened. Add remaining ingredients and heat. May be served hot from a thermos or cold with hot/cold meats or vegetables.

Caper Sauce

1/2 c sour cream
1/2 c mayonnaise
3 T milk

2 T capers (chopped)
1 T parsley (chopped)
1 tsp Dijon-style mustard

With a wire whip, combine all ingredients to a smooth consistency. Cover and refrigerate until ready for use. May be served hot or cold over hot/cold chicken breast, shrimp, fish or vegetables such as broccoli, asparagus, etc.

Seafarer Sauce or Salad Dressing

Makes: 2 c

2 cloves garlic (crushed)
1 c yogurt
½ c tomato catsup
1 tsp prepared horseradish
1 tsp white wine Worcestershire
  sauce

1 tsp pepper
¼ tsp Tabasco sauce
¼ tsp paprika
2 T onion (minced)
1 tsp Dijon-style mustard

In a covered container, mix ingredients together and refrigerate until service. This sauce can be used as a dip for raw vegetables and seafood or as a salad dressing.

Homemade Tartar Sauce for a Lot

Makes: 1½ qt

1 qt mayonnaise
1 c relish
1 T Worcestershire sauce
⅓ c fresh squeezed lemon juice

⅓ bunch parsley (chopped)
1 T paprika
¼ tsp curry
¼ tsp dill

In a covered container, mix all ingredients and keep refrigerated until service.

Cranberry Orange Relish

Makes: 1 1/2 c

1 bag fresh cranberries (rinsed)
1 orange (peel only)
1 c sugar

In a food processor with metal blade, combine all ingredients and process until everything is chopped to relish consistency. Refrigerate and serve with turkey, duck or chicken. This is really easy but delicious.

BREADS
AND DESSERTS

Sesame Orange Banana Bread
Makes: 1 loaf

2 c flour
½ c instant potatoes
1 T baking powder
½ tsp salt
⅓ c sugar
¼ c butter or margarine
   (softened)
1 egg
½ tsp cinnamon

¼ tsp nutmeg
2 T orange juice (concentrated)
¾ c milk
2 T sesame seeds
1 c banana (mashed)
2 T orange peel (grated)
½ c walnuts, almonds or pecans
   (chopped)

In a mixing bowl, combine flour, baking powder, salt, sugar and spices. Mix remaining ingredients in a separate bowl and blend with dry ingredients until moistened. Spoon into a greased loaf pan and bake about 1 hour at 350 degrees. Cool for 10 minutes, then run a knife around edges and remove bread from pan. This bread may be frozen ahead then served toasted with butter and marmalade.

California Avocado Bread
Makes: 1 loaf

2 c flour
1 c sugar
1 tsp baking powder
¼ tsp salt
1 egg
½ c avocado (1 medium)
½ c banana (1 medium)

½ c buttermilk or regular milk
½ c margarine (softened)
⅓ c coconut
¼-½ c raisins or chopped dates
¾ c walnuts, almonds or pecans
   (chopped)

Mix together flour, sugar, baking powder and salt in a bowl and set aside. Using a blender or food processor mix egg, avocado, banana, buttermilk and margarine until smooth. Combine avocado mixture with dry ingredients and stir until moistened. Add remaining ingredients and spoon into a greased loaf pan. Bake at 350 degrees for 1 hour or until toothpick comes out clean. Freezes well.

Variation: For muffins, fill 12 muffin papers ⅔ full and bake at 350 degrees for 20-30 minutes.

Victory Muffins

Makes: 1 dozen

2 cups flour
¼ c sugar
3 tsp baking powder
½ tsp salt

1 c milk
⅓ c vegetable oil
1 egg (beaten)

Sift together dry ingredients and set aside. In a mixing bowl, beat together milk, oil and egg until thoroughly combined. Make a well in the center of the flour mixture and add milk mixture all at once. Stir quickly until batter is moistened but still lumpy. Pour batter into greased muffin cups or muffin papers and bake at 400 degrees for 20-25 minutes.

Variations: Add ½ c nuts, blueberries or fruit.

Rye-Soy Muffins

Makes: 12

1½ c rye flour
½ c soy flour (stir before
    measuring)
¼ c bran
1 T baking powder
1 T caraway, sesame or poppy
    seed

1 c walnuts or pecans (chopped)
¾ tsp salt
1¼ c water
1 egg (lightly beaten)
2 T honey
2 T oil

In mixing bowl, combine flours, bran, baking powder, seeds, nuts and salt. Separately mix water, egg, honey and oil. Blend into flour mixture until just moistened. Divide into greased or paper-lined muffin pans and bake at 350 degrees for 25 minutes or until browned.

Apple Oatmeal Bread

Makes: 1 loaf

2 medium apples (peeled, cored
    and coarse chopped)
2½ c flour
1 c sugar
1 T baking powder
1 tsp salt

1 tsp cinnamon
1 c regular oats
1 c walnuts or pecans (chopped)
2 eggs (beaten)
1 c milk
¼ c oil

Microwave or use a saucepan to heat apples for 8 minutes, until softened. In a large bowl, stir together flour, sugar, baking powder, salt, cinnamon, oats and nuts. In a separate bowl combine eggs, milk and oil. Stir this into flour mixture, add apples and mix until all ingredients are moistened. Pour into greased loaf pan and bake at 350 degrees for 50-60 minutes or until a toothpick comes out clean. Cool 10 minutes and remove from pan. Cool thoroughly, wrap, refrigerate or freeze till ready for service. Try this one with cream cheese or toasted with butter.

Pumpkin Bread

Makes: 3 loaves

4 c pumpkin (or a 1 lb 13 oz can)
2 c sugar
2 c packed brown sugar
1 c oil
1 tsp salt
1 tsp cloves

2 tsp cinnamon
4 tsp soda
1 tsp vanilla
5 c flour
1 c nuts (chopped)

Mix ingredients in order and fill 3 greased loaf pans ½ full of batter. Bake at 350 degrees for 1 hour or till toothpick comes out clean.

Remove from baking pans and cool before service.

Pineapple Rum Bread

Makes: 1 loaf

2 c flour
1 T baking powder
½ tsp salt
1 c sugar
½ c butter or margarine
  (softened)
2 eggs (beaten)
2 bananas (mashed)

1 (8 oz) can crushed pineapple
  with juice
grated rind of 1 lemon
2 T rum
¼ c milk
⅓ c coconut
1 c walnuts (chopped)

Sift dry ingredients and set aside. In a separate bowl, mix together butter, eggs, bananas, pineapple, lemon rind, rum and milk. Stir in coconut and nuts. Spoon into a WELL-buttered loaf pan and bake at 350 degrees for 1 hour. Cool for 10 minutes then loosen sides from pan and turn out. Wrap for freezing or to take to the game hot.

Persimmon Bread

1 c packed brown sugar
1 c flour
1 1/2 tsp baking soda
2 tsp cinnamon
1/4 tsp cloves
1/4 c mace

1 c persimmon pulp (mashed)
1/2 c milk
1 egg (slightly beaten)
1/2 c currants or raisins
3/4 c walnuts (chopped)

Sift together dry ingredients and add persimmon, milk and egg. Mix until moistened then add currants and nuts. Bake in a greased loaf pan at 350 degrees for 40 minutes. This is a pudding-type bread so is very soft and moist. Cool for 5-10 minutes before removing from pan. Carefully run a knife around edge of pan and turn out of pan.

Variation: Serve with cognac glaze given below.

2-3 c butter or margarine (softened)
1/4 tsp nutmeg
2 c powdered sugar
2 T cognac or brandy

Cream together butter and nutmeg. Add sugar and cognac. Blend until smooth. Spread over warm bread, cool and wrap.

Nordic Bread

Makes: 2 loaves

1³/₄ c milk (scalded)
2 tsp salt
¹/₃ c vegetable oil
¹/₃ c brown sugar
¹/₂ c water

2 eggs
2 T dry yeast
2 c whole wheat flour
2 c pastry flour
2 c rye flour

For this recipe you need a standup mixer with a dough-hook, or tons of time to knead. Pour slightly-cooled milk into mixer bowl and add salt, oil, brown sugar, water, eggs and yeast. Mix the three flours together and add 3 cups to milk mixture. Blend ingredients and add 3 more cups of flour. Use dough-hook to knead 7-10 minutes. Cover with a towel and let rise until doubled. Knead briefly to remove air from dough (about 2 minutes). Form into loaves and place in a well-oiled pan. Let rise again until about double and brush top of loaf with melted butter or oil. Bake for approximately 1 hour at 350 degrees.

Note: The melted butter will make the loaves crusty on the outside, but for dieters the same can be done by placing a pan of water in the bottom of the oven during baking. You can also slice X's in the top for a more decorative look. This is great bread for making a meal at any event.

Holiday Eggnog Bread

Makes: 1 loaf

2³/₄ c flour
³/₄ c sugar
1 T baking powder
1 tsp salt
³/₄ tsp nutmeg
¹/₄ tsp mace
¹/₂ tsp cinnamon

¹/₄ c butter or margarine (melted)
2 eggs (separated)
1¹/₂ c half & half
¹/₄ c rum or brandy
³/₄ c walnuts or pecans (chopped)
³/₄ c candied fruit

In a large mixing bowl, sift dry ingredients and set aside. Mix together butter, egg yolks, cream, and brandy. In a separate bowl, beat egg whites until stiff. Add egg white and yolk mixture to flour, stirring until just moistened. Fold in nuts and candied fruit. Spoon into a greased loaf pan and bake 1 hour at 350 degrees or until toothpick comes out clean. This is a festive item around the holidays.

Chewy Chocolate Chip Bars
Makes: 32

Bars
1 c butter or margarine
3 c brown sugar (packed)
2 c flour

Topping
4 eggs (beaten)
1 T vanilla
4 T flour
2 tsp baking powder
1 tsp salt
2 c walnuts or pecans (chopped)
1 (12 oz) bag semi-sweet chocolate chips

In a medium mixing bowl, cream together butter and 1 c brown sugar. Mix in 2 c flour until blended. Pat this dough evenly into the bottom of a greased 9x13 inch baking pan. Bake at 350 degrees for 10 minutes and cool.

In same mixing bowl, beat together eggs, remaining brown sugar, vanilla, 4 T flour, baking powder, salt and chopped nuts. Spread this mixture over dough in baking pan. Sprinkle with chocolate chips and bake at 350 degrees for 25 minutes or until golden brown. Cool and cut into 32 bars. These are really rich, so cut small pieces.

Mocha Maniac Ice Cream Pie

Serves: 10-12

4 squares semi-sweet chocolate
1 cube butter
4½ c bran flake cereal

½ gallon almond mocha fudge
  ice cream
½ c slivered almonds

In a medium saucepan, melt chocolate and butter over low heat. Add bran flakes and mix well. Spread mixture into a buttered 9 inch deep-dish pie pan. Put into freezer for about 15-20 minutes or until firm. Meanwhile, soften ice cream. Spoon into pie shell and top with almonds. Freeze until firm. For service, cut frozen pie with a sharp knife or pie server. Dunk knife in warm water between cuts for easier service.

Variations:
1. Just about anything!! Vanilla ice cream with strawberry topping or fresh fruit.
2. Chocolate mint ice cream topped with chocolate chips.
3. Around the holidays, vanilla ice cream with crushed peppermint sticks.

Strawberry Zabaione

Serves: 4

2 baskets fresh strawberries
  (cleaned and stemmed)
4 egg yolks
4 T sugar
¾ c Marsala wine

½ tsp vanilla
¼ c whipping cream (slightly
  whipped)
slivered almonds

Chill strawberries until ready for use. On top of a double boiler above simmering water, wire whip egg yolks, sugar, Marsala and vanilla together until fluffy. Add cream. Continue whipping until slightly thickened. May take up to ten minutes. Cover and refrigerate. To serve, place strawberries in stemmed glasses or in individual bowls and top with Zabaione sauce and slivered almonds.

Scratch Cheesecake

Serves: 8-12

Crust
1 c graham cracker crumbs
¼ c almonds (chopped fine)

⅓ c sugar
½ c butter or margarine (melted)

Combine all ingredients and mold into a 9 inch pie pan or cheesecake pan with removable bottom. Chill 45 minutes or about as long as it takes to get the filling ready.

Filling
2 pkg (8 oz each) cream cheese
  (softened)
½ c sugar
2 eggs

½ tsp almond extract
8 oz sour cream
2-3 T sugar

In a food processor or by hand, beat together cream cheese, sugar, eggs and almond extract until smooth. Pour into crust and bake 25-35 minutes at 350 degrees. Center should begin to look firm. In a separate bowl, mix sour cream with 2-3 T of sugar. Smooth this mixture over cream cheese layer and bake an additional 10-12 minutes at 375 degrees. Chill until ready for service. Can be topped with fresh fruit, pie topping or crushed pineapple or served plain sprinkled with additional chopped almonds.

Cream Puff Pie

Serves: 6-8

½ c flour
dash of salt
1 tsp sugar
½ c milk
2 T butter or margarine
2 large eggs (to be at room
   temperature)

Filling
2 eggs
3 T sugar
3 T rum
1 (12 oz) bag chocolate chips
1½ c milk (heated almost to
   boiling point)
1 c whipped cream
½ c pecans (chopped)

Preheat oven to 400 degrees. In a mixing bowl, stir first 3 ingredients. Heat milk and butter in a heavy pan and bring to a boil. Add all flour in one fell swoop and vigorously whip with a wooden spoon until smooth. Beat until mixture does not cling to sides of pan. Remove from heat and let set for 1-2 minutes. Add one egg at a time and beat until no longer slimy. Put mixture into a greased pie tin and cook at 400 degrees for 10 minutes. Reduce heat to 350 degrees and continue to cook about 20 minutes or until firm to touch. Prick center with a fork and let cool. For filling, place all ingredients except whipped cream and nuts in a blender. Blend 1 minute at low speed. Pour into cream puff shell and chill 4-6 hours. Serve topped with whipped cream and nuts.

Variations:
1. Fill with whatever you like. Try pudding or fresh fruit.
2. Fill with crab or shrimp spread surrounded by fresh vegetables and crackers.

Pine Nut Torte

Crust
2 T sugar
1 c flour
6 T butter or margarine
1 egg
¼ c apricot, strawberry or
   raspberry jam

Filling
1 can (8 oz) almond paste
6 eggs (separated)
¼ c sugar
¼ c flour
¾ tsp baking powder
¾ c toasted pine nuts

To prepare crust, mix sugar and flour in a bowl. Add butter and cut into fine crumbs with a pastry cutter or fork. Stir in egg. Press into a ball and roll out to a 12-13 inch diameter. Fit into a 10 inch cake pan or a cheese cake pan with a removable bottom. Press dough into pan and spread bottom with jam.

In a food processor or with an electric mixer, combine almond paste with egg yolks, sugar, flour and baking powder, until smooth. Whip egg whites to soft peaks and fold ½ of these into almond paste mixture. Fold in remaining egg white and pine nuts.

Pour batter into prepared crust. Bake at 350 degrees for 35 minutes or until firm. Cool slightly and run a knife around pan rim. Wrap and refrigerate. For service, remove pan rim and place on a serving platter.

Variations:
1. No pine nuts? Use chopped almonds or walnuts.
2. Top with fresh fruit like raspberries and whipped cream before serving.

Health Nut Cake

1 c salad oil
1 c brown sugar
1 c white sugar
4 eggs
2 c flour
1 tsp baking soda
1 tsp baking powder

½ tsp cinnamon
½ tsp salt
1 c walnuts or pecans
1 c carrot (grated)
1 c zucchini (grated)
10 oz pkg frozen spinach
    (thawed and squeezed dry)

In a large mixing bowl, beat oil, sugars and eggs together. Add dry ingredients and mix well. Stir in nuts, carrots, zucchini and spinach. Pour into tube pan, sheet cake pan or 2 layer cake pans. Bake for 40 minutes at 350 degrees or until toothpick comes out clean. Cake may be served plain or with cream cheese frosting below.

Frosting

1 cube butter or margarine
    (softened)
8 oz cream cheese (softened)

2 T orange juice concentrate
1 box powdered sugar
2 T grated orange peel

Cream butter, cream cheese, orange juice, sugar and peel together. Apply to cool cake. Garnish with walnut halves and more grated orange peel. Parsley on top or alongside is an appropriate garnish, too!!

Pineapple Cake

Serves: 8-10

1 can pineapple (crushed)
2 c flour
2 c sugar
2 eggs
1 tsp baking soda
1 tsp salt
½ c walnuts or pecans (chopped)
½ c coconut

Cream Cheese Frosting
8 oz pkg cream cheese (softened)
1 cube butter or margarine
  (softened)
2½ c powdered sugar
1 tsp vanilla
toasted coconut and whole nuts

To prepare cake, mix all ingredients and pour into a 9x11 inch cake pan. Bake 45 minutes at 300 degrees. While cake is baking prepare frosting by beating all ingredients, except coconut and nuts, until smooth. Frost warm cake with cream cheese frosting and sprinkle with toasted coconut and whole nuts.

Raceteam Special

Serves: 6-8

½ cube butter or margarine
⅓ c brown sugar (packed) or
  honey
½ c orange juice concentrate

1 tsp vanilla extract
6 large bananas (sliced
  lengthwise)
2 oz coconut (shredded)

In a small sauce pan, heat butter, sugar, orange juice and vanilla over medium heat until warm, or about 4-5 minutes. Do Not Boil. Place bananas in a lightly-buttered covered casserole dish. Sprinkle coconut over bananas and drizzle with brown sugar mixture. Bake at 375 degrees for approximately 15 minutes. This is sinful winter or summer but is really good just scooped over vanilla ice cream. May be garnished with ⅓ c slivered almonds and whipped cream.

Raspberry Coffee Cake

3 to 3½ c flour
1 pkg dry yeast
1 tsp salt
¾ c milk (warm)
¼ c oil
¼ c sugar

2 eggs
½ c raspberry jam
1 c powdered sugar
¼ tsp almond extract
milk
¼ c slivered or chopped almonds

In a large mixing bowl, combine 2 c flour, yeast and salt. Add milk, oil, sugar and eggs. Beat with an electric mixer for 3 minutes, scraping bowl occasionally. With a spoon stir in as much remaining flour as possible. On a lightly floured board, knead for about 5-7 minutes or until elastic. Place into a greased bowl and cover for 1 hour or until doubled.

Punch bread down and roll out into a large rectangle about 1 inch thick. Make 1 inch diagonal cuts along the longest edges of the bread that extend ⅓ way into the center. Spread raspberry jam across the center of the bread. Weave and twist the outer strips of the bread over the filling to form a criss cross effect. Carefully slide coffee cake off onto a greased baking sheet. Let rise in a warm area until doubled (about 45-60 minutes). Bake at 375 degrees for 25-30 minutes. Combine sugar, almond extract and enough milk to form a thick pourable glaze. Drizzle over bread, sprinkle with chopped almonds and garnish with fresh raspberries. This coffee cake is an elegant addition to a pregame brunch when served on a silver tray or antique (possibly not so antique) piece of china.

Cinnamon Sour Cream Coffee Cake

Serves: 8-10

1 c butter or margarine
1¼ c sugar
2 eggs
¼ c buttermilk
½ c sour cream
1 tsp vanilla

2 c flour
½ tsp baking soda
1½ tsp baking powder
¾ c chopped almonds or walnuts
(mix with 2 tsp cinnamon and
2 T sugar)

Grease and flour a 9 inch bundt or tube pan. In a large mixing bowl, combine butter, sugar and eggs. Beat until fluffy, then blend in buttermilk, sour cream and vanilla. Sift together dry ingredients and add to sour cream mixture. Spoon ½ of batter into pan and sprinkle with ½ of nut mixture. Spoon over remaining batter. Bake for 45-50 minutes at 350 degrees.

Note: Coffee cake may be made ahead, refrigerated overnight and baked the next morning.

Date Nut Cake

Serves: 12-15

Filling
1/2 lb pitted dates (chopped)
1/2 c brown sugar
1 c water
1/2 c walnuts or pecans (chopped)

Cake
3/4 c butter or margarine
1 c sugar
2 eggs
2 c flour
1 1/2 c rolled oats
1/2 c flaked coconut
1 tsp baking soda

Boil filling ingredients until dates are soft. Remove from heat and set aside to cool. In a mixing bowl, cream together butter and sugar. Stir in eggs. Add flour, oats, coconut and baking soda. Blend completely and press 1/2 of the mixture into a well-greased 8x12 inch pan. Layer with filling and crumble remaining cake mixture on top. Bake at 325 degrees for about 30 minutes or until browned. This is rich and excellent topped with whipped cream. It can also be made ahead and frozen.

Fresh Fruit in Champagne

Makes: 1 qt

4 c peeled pears, seedless grapes, tangerine sections, plums, quartered kiwi, strawberries, nectarines or a combination of your favorite fruits.

1/2 c sugar
1 1/2 c chilled Rhine wine
2 T pineapple juice concentrate
1 1/2 c chilled champagne

Mix all ingredients except champagne and chill until ready for use. Just before serving add chilled champagne to fruit and serve. This is very pretty in tall stemmed glasses and is a wonderful beginning for a brunch-type tailgate or after a heavy meal.

Make at the Game Vanilla Ice Cream with Grand Marnier Strawberry Sauce

Makes: 2 qts

1 (14 oz) can condensed milk
1³/₄ c water
3 eggs (beaten)
2 c heavy cream
2¹/₂ tsp vanilla
ice and rock salt

Sauce
2 pints fresh strawberries or raspberries (cleaned)
1 tsp fresh lemon juice
5 T powdered sugar
1-2 T Grand Marnier

The night before service, in the top of a double boiler over simmering water, combine milk and water. Beat until smooth and stir a small amount of milk into beaten eggs. Add beaten egg mixture to milk and simmer, stirring constantly until mixture thickens slightly. Remove from heat and refrigerate to cool to room temperature. Stir in cream and vanilla. Chill until ready for use.

To prepare sauce, mash most of strawberries and add remaining ingredients. Blend well and refrigerate until ready for use.

3-4 hours before service pour ice cream mixture into the top of a crank or electric ice cream maker. Fill tub completely with ice and sprinkle with rock salt. Use about 6 parts ice to 1 part salt. Churn 20 minutes and add salt and ice as it melts. Keep churning until ice cream is at a smooth consistency, then add more ice and salt and let stand for 2 or more hours. For service, scoop out ice cream and top with Grand Marnier sauce.

BEVERAGES

The Fun Hog

Makes: 1 (That's all you need)

1 shot (1 oz) green chartreuse
1 shot 151 rum

1 small glass
1 strong stomach

Into a small glass pour 1 shot green charteuse and then float rum on top. That's it, watch it from here!

Simple Blended Daiquiris

Serves: 6-8

1 (6 oz) can frozen limeade
  concentrate
6 oz light rum
1 T sugar

1 ice cube tray of ice
1-2 drops green food coloring,
  if desired

In a blender container, frappé limeade concentrate, rum, sugar, ice and food color until smooth and free of lumps. Pour into tall glasses and garnish with a lime slice.

Sunday Morning Wake-Up

Makes: 6

4 oz amaretto liqueur
2 oz Grand Marnier

4 c hot French Roast coffee
whipped cream

Combine all ingredients except whipped cream and transport to game in a thermos. Serve hot at gametime in mugs topped with whipped cream.

Rose Cooler

4 c white wine
1 c pink lemonade concentrate

2 c soda water
½ c Grenadine

Combine all ingredients and pour over crushed ice. Garnish with a red rose and lemon wedge along the upper lip of the glass. This drink alone is enough to turn the tide of any game!!

Scotch Toddy

Serves: 4-6

3 c boiling water
2 T honey or brown sugar
½ tsp ground nutmeg

6 oz scotch
juice of 2 lemons

Dissolve honey or sugar in boiling water and add remaining ingredients. Stir and serve hot or pour into a preheated thermos. May be garnished at gametime with a lemon twist.

Thermos Bloody Marys

Makes: 2½ qts

64 oz tomato juice
¼ c Worcestershire sauce
3¾ to 4 c vodka
juice of 3 lemons

1 T Tabasco sauce to taste
salt and pepper to taste
3 tsp prepared horseradish
fresh celery and lemon slices

Mix all ingredients (except celery and lemon slices) in a chilled thermos. Serve at gametime over ice and garnish with celery sticks and fresh lemon slices.

Hot Lemon Brandy

Serves: 8

¼ c sugar
½ c lemon juice
1½ T butter
4 c water

1 c brandy
½ tsp lemon peel (grated)
½ tsp orange peel (grated)
cinnamon sticks

In a saucepan, heat all ingredients and serve in mugs with a cinnamon stick.

Raspberry Twist

Serves: 8

1 (10 oz) pkg frozen raspberries
1 (6 oz) can lemonade concentrate
1 c vodka

4 c ice cubes
3 T sugar

Put all ingredients into blender and blend until slushy. Serve in tall stemmed glasses garnished with mint.

Blended Oregon Sprintzers

Serves: 8

5 c club soda
3 T Rose's lime juice
8 oz frozen raspberries
6 oz gin

¼ c frozen apple juice
  (concentrate)
1 tray ice cubes
8 mint sprigs for garnish

Mix all ingredients (except ice and mint). Pour into tall glasses of ice and garnish with a mint sprig. I also like this done with crushed pineapple.

Frozen Peach Daiquiri

Serves: 6

4 fresh peaches (peeled and pitted)
2 c limeade (made from
   concentrate)

¾ c rum
½ c peach brandy
1 tray ice cubes

Put all ingredients into blender and blend for about 30 seconds or until all lumps are gone. May be garnished with a sprig of mint or lime slices.

Spiced Coffee

Serves: 8

8-9 c hot strong coffee
2 cinnamon sticks
3 whole cloves

1 orange peel (cut into strips)
1 c Anisette liquor
brown sugar to taste

Pour all ingredients into a preheated thermos and let steep until game time. Pour coffee into mugs and let it warm you to your toes.

Sea Sips

½ tsp celery salt
salt and pepper to taste
6 oz gin or vodka
2½ c tomato juice

1 c clam juice
juice of 2 limes
1 tsp horseradish

Mix all ingredients and pour over ice. May be garnished with a lime wedge. Outstanding when served with oyster crackers and seafood dip for the America's Cup.

Hot Spiked Cider

Serves: 6-8

½ gallon apple cider
1½ c White Zinfandel

1 tsp pumpkin pie spice
6-8 cinnamon sticks

In a large saucepan, heat all ingredients (except cinnamon sticks) until hot. Serve hot in mugs garnished with a cinnamon stick or pour into a preheated thermos till gametime.

Hot Tomato Fumble

Serves: 4

1 (16 oz) can tomato sauce
1 can chicken consommé
1 fresh tomato (chopped)
2 green onions

1 T fresh ginger (grated)
½ c vodka
salt and Tabasco to taste

In a saucepan, heat all ingredients (except vodka) to a boil. Pour hot mixture and vodka into a preheated thermos and serve hot at gametime with a stalk of celery, pickled string bean or spear of marinated asparagus as a swizzle stick.

Apricot Nog

Serves: 6

2 c apricot nectar
2 eggs
6 oz vodka or gin
½ c frozen pineapple juice
　concentrate

1 c powdered milk
3 c ice
6 sprigs fresh mint leaves

Blend all ingredients in blender until frothy. May be garnished with fresh mint or an orange slice.

Denver Orange Crush

Serves: 4-6

2 c grapefruit juice
1 c orange juice
½ c lemon juice
2 T sugar

½ c tequila
2 oz white wine
ice

Blend in a blender until frothy or shake in a shaker with crushed ice. Garnish with lemon and strawberrry on a drinking straw.

Jamaican Javelin

Serves: 4-6

6 oz rum
4 T maple syrup
juice of 2 limes
¼ c orange juice concentrate

1 oz Benedictine
1 T Angostura Bitters
1½ to 2 c crushed ice

Combine all ingredients in blender and liquify. Pour into a chilled thermos and shake well before serving at gametime.

172

Mulled Wine

Serves: 8

1 orange
1 lemon
1 (750 ml) bottle dry red wine
¼ c sugar

1 cinnamon stick
¼ tsp ground nutmeg
¼ tsp pie spice
6-8 whole cloves

Peel orange and lemon, cutting off the white membrane as close to the skin as possible. Retain the skin and slice into thin strips. Combine wine, sugar, peel, cinnamon, nutmeg, pie spice and cloves in a saucepan and simmer for about 5 minutes or until hot. Serve hot into mugs or pour into a preheated thermos. May be garnished with orange or lemon peel studded with whole cloves.

Cranberry Champagne Cocktail

Serves: 10

5 c cranberry juice
1 c pineapple juice
1 fifth champagne

½ c cognac
crushed ice
orange slices

Mix cranberry juice, pineapple juice and cognac together in a thermos till gametime. For service, mix in champagne and pour into glasses of crushed ice. Garnish with an orange slice.

The Blue & Gold

Serves: 4

10 drops blue curacao
2 c club soda

6 oz vodka
4 twists lemon

In a container, combine blue curacao and vodka. Pour evenly into 4 glasses of crushed ice and add ½ c soda water to each. Garnish with a lemon twist.

INDEX

Index

Sandwiches

Sauces

Soups

Soups — Continued

Order Form

To order additional copies of The All-American Sports Fan Cookbook, send $9.95 plus $2.50 for postage and handling to:

Sports Fan Cookbook
425 Main St.
Murphy's, California 95247

- -

Name_____

Address_____

City, State, Zip_____

_____ copies @ $9.95 each_____

$2.50 shipping and handling_____

TOTAL_____

- -

Name_____

Address_____

City, State, Zip_____

_____ copies @ $9.95 each_____

$2.50 shipping and handling_____

TOTAL_____